Growing Flowers

Growing Flowers

Everything You Need to Know about Planting,
Tending, Harvesting and Arranging Beautiful Blooms

Niki Irving

Flourish Flower Farm

yellow pear press

An imprint of Mango Publishing

CORAL GABLES

Cover Design: Elina Diaz
Cover Photo/illustration: Niki Irving
Photography: Julia Berolzheimer, Sarah Collier, Tonya Engelbrecht, Niki Irving and Meghan Rolfe
Layout & Design: Elina Diaz

For permission requests, please contact the publisher at:
Mango Publishing Group
2850 S Douglas Road, 2nd Floor
Coral Gables, FL 33134 USA
info@mango.bz

For special orders, quantity sales, course adoptions and corporate sales, please email the publisher at sales@mango.bz. For trade and wholesale sales, please contact Ingram Publisher Services at customer.service@ingramcontent.com or +1.800.509.4887.

Growing Flowers: Everything You Need to Know about Planting, Tending, Harvesting and Arranging Beautiful Blooms

Library of Congress Cataloging-in-Publication number: Pending
ISBN: (print) 978-1-64250-550-4, (ebook) 978-1-64250-551-1
BISAC category code: GAR004000, GARDENING / Flowers / General

Printed in the United States of America

For Mom and Dad,

who shared their love of nature

and the gratification that comes

from a good day's work in the garden.

Table of Contents

Foreword **Growing Flowers...for All Seasons** **13**

Introduction **The Story of Flourish Flower Farm** **17**
    How I Became a Flower Farmer 17
    Flourishing 21

Chapter 1 **Know Your Climate** **25**
    About Hardiness Zones 26
    Freezing Temperatures 29
    Growing Climates 30

Chapter 2 **Choosing and Preparing a Garden Plot** **33**
    Growing Organically 33
    Laying Out a Garden Plot 34
    Soil Preparation 36
    All About Soil 40
    Adding Compost 43

Chapter 3 **Planning What to Plant** **47**
    Measuring Your Garden Plot 47
    Crop Planning 52
    Days to Maturity 54
    Plant Hardiness 56
    Repeat Bloomers and One-Stem Bloomers 59
    Succession Planting 60
    Planting for a Balanced Garden Bouquet 62
    Ordering Seeds and Bulbs 63

Chapter 4 **Seed Starting and Planting** **67**
    Creating an Indoor Grow Station 68
    Growing and Caring for Seedlings 70
    Transplanting into the Garden 71
    Planting Bulbs 73

Chapter 5 **Tending the Garden** **83**
    Weeding 83
    Irrigation 89
    Fertilizing 90
    Plant Support 91

Pinching..92

Common Diseases Affecting Flowers...93

Beneficial Insects...95

Common Garden Pests..97

Chapter 6 **Harvesting and Arranging Flowers**   **101**

Harvesting..103

Deadheading...104

Arranging...105

Chapter 7 **Putting the Garden to Bed**   **123**

Garden Bed Cleanup..123

Composting..124

Cover Crops...127

Deep Dive: Digging Dahlia Tubers...130

Other Fall Garden Chores..131

Keep Growing Flowers   **135**

Tools   **136**

Resources   **41**

Acknowledgements   **144**

About the Author   **146**

Index   **148**

Foreword

Growing Flowers... for All Seasons

In my writing courses, one of the first prompts I give students is: *Describe your earliest memory of encountering a flower, a garden, or nature.* Everyone has an answer, and, because it's entirely personal, I find that students (flower farmers, florists, designers, and gardeners) forget their writing anxieties and let their stories flow from their hearts to the page. Sentence by sentence, the touching narratives are frequently connected to equally poignant family memories.

So I'll tell you mine: my earliest floral encounters took place during my late-1960s summers in the Hammond, Indiana, backyard of my maternal grandparents, Helen and Daniel Ford. "Grand-dad," as we called my mom's father, planted County Fair-worthy, prizewinning dahlias in a raised bed that ran parallel to the narrow concrete walkway from the back porch to the alley gate. Like thespians in a play, the hybrid blooms put on a polychromatic production, planted by height (and all towering above my head). Today, decades later, I strive to recreate that childhood wonderment in my own dahlia patch.

There is a parallel between my story and that of Nicolette "Niki" Irving, the young woman who shares her beautiful floral journey in the pages of *Growing Flowers*. Niki turned her dream into a fulfilling and creative life rooted in the land where she farms in Asheville, North Carolina, not far from where she

grew up. Like many of us whose paths have taken us far from home, through many other adventures both personal and professional, Niki's life has come full circle and returned her to her origins. She draws from a childhood in which plants were a constant presence, thanks to her family's landscaping and nursery business. As a young woman, Niki's first career in outdoor travel continued to connect her with the natural world. Now, with her husband William, she is steward of a nine-acre, specialty cut flower farm in the Blue Ridge Mountains. Flourish Flower Farm keeps Niki ever close to the soil, as she tends to more than three hundred botanical varieties that supply wedding and event clients, floral CSA subscribers, local grocery stores, and other design clients in her community.

Living among the flowers she grows, and from which Nikki and her family derive a livelihood, is the embodiment of Slow Flowers, a philosophy and movement that I launched with the publication of my book *Slow Flowers* (St. Lynn's Press, 2013). I met Niki when she joined Slow Flowers Society, our community of flower farmers, florists, and practitioners committed to saving domestic floral agriculture. I've featured her in articles about both her designs and the way she educates consumers about the importance of local and sustainably grown flowers. Now, with her new book, *Growing Flowers*, Niki generously shares her knowledge with a much larger audience of floral enthusiasts, home gardeners, and aspiring flower farmers. You are in good hands!

A self-described farmer-florist, Niki brings a designer's eye to what she plants, tends, and harvests. Over the past five years, she has personally taught more than five hundred students at Flourish Flower Farm workshops and during one-on-one intensives. She encourages her students to hone dual skill sets of *growing* flowers and *designing* with them. And now, all that workshop content is available to you.

Think of this book as a personal workshop that you can return to again and again. Through these beautiful and engaging pages, you'll find Niki's dream and lifestyle irresistible. I believe her story and her generosity of knowledge will inspire you to follow your dream of living a more creative life.

Like her Flourish Flower Farm workshops, Niki will introduce you to unique and surprising seasonal varieties that you can grow yourself. As you establish a personal cutting garden (dare we say, a micro flower farm?), she covers everything from knowing your climate to choosing a site. She shares advice on what to plant, as well as how to start seeds, tend your flower garden, and harvest at just the right stage. Once you harvest those stems, the floral artistry begins, as Niki teaches you how to arrange centerpieces and bouquets using her basic design principles and step-by-step tips.

Do you dream of creating a flower garden? As you grow, arrange, and enjoy flowers in your home, give bouquets as gifts, and beautify the world outside your windows, you'll gain confidence and lifelong skills. Embrace a flower-filled life as you dig deep into *Growing Flowers*.

Debra Prinzing is the founder and creative director of **Slow Flowers Society**. Her most recent book is *Slow Flowers Journal–Volume One*. (You can see some of Niki's bouquets in the "Slow Weddings" chapter!)

Introduction

The Story of Flourish Flower Farm

For as long as I can remember, I have always loved flowers. They have the ability to communicate such a vast array of emotions: romantic love, friendship, self-love, remorse, condolences, celebration, and "just because." The "just because" is my personal favorite, since we all need more beauty in our daily lives. Beauty is a language all its own, and I believe that it is one of caring. There really is no greater joy than handing someone a bouquet of flowers that I grew myself and watching their face light up. Whether you are growing flowers to admire them, to give away to friends and family, or in hopes of creating a flower farming business, this book is designed to provide you with concrete advice on how to get started growing flowers.

How I Became a Flower Farmer

I grew up on the coast of South Carolina. Some of my earliest memories are of climbing the giant magnolia trees outside of my dad's office and picking flowers from my mom's garden. My parents are both plant-loving and plant-growing people, so I suppose a green thumb is in my DNA. At a young age, my mom taught me the joy of picking lettuce from the garden to make salad for dinner. I spent hours every summer watering trees at my dad's plant nursery and landscaping company, and I wanted to be just like him when I grew up. Family vacations were spent camping in the same mountains that I now call home. It's no wonder that my heart led me to grow plants here in the Blue Ridge Mountains.

I spent my twenties living and adventuring in the Western United States while leading outdoor adventure trips for teens. I would save all my money—easy to do when you're basically living in a tent—in order to travel and do the same activities (without the company of teenagers) in places like Nepal, Peru, New Zealand, and Costa Rica. I also apprenticed on an organic farm and fell in love with farming. But the mountains were still calling my name, so I eventually became the director of an outdoor education program. After about ten years of traveling while leading outdoor adventure trips, I started to crave a real home. I bought a little bungalow in the heart of Asheville, adopted a dog and cat, raised some chickens, and built a huge garden. Around that same time, I reconnected with William, a college friend who had recently moved to Asheville. After a few months of renewing our friendship, we fell in love and got married.

Although my home life was nearly perfect, I started to feel restless in my professional life and was being drawn even more strongly toward farming. I knew deep down that I wanted to grow plants, to cultivate and harvest, but vegetables didn't feel like the right place to start. One day while trail running, I had an intense vision that I needed to grow flowers. I could see it so clearly in my mind: fields full of flowers and me tending them. Throughout my life, I've carried along my parents' love of flowering plants—drooling over dahlias at Pike's Place Market in Seattle, always having vases of fresh flowers in the house, even designing the flowers for my wedding. I tentatively approached William, who by now was well aware of my professional restlessness and wild dreams, and told him that I wanted to become a flower farmer. I read everything I could get my hands on, researched endlessly, wrote a business plan, and created financial projections. I spent every spare moment developing this dream. The biggest obstacle was that I couldn't imagine building this new business and really giving it 100 percent while working a full-time job off the farm. I wanted to go all-in on this dream, and William gave me his full support.

So we made a plan: we tapped into our savings, I tearfully left my job, and we found some beautiful land to lease. Leaving behind a steady paycheck, health insurance, set work hours, and the camaraderie of coworkers felt like such a huge risk. I was absolutely terrified! But I knew that in order to make this dream happen, I would have to focus, be organized, and work harder than I could imagine.

We humans crave beauty in our lives. Flowers truly feed the soul and are such a unique expression of caring. I love telling people the romantic names of the flower varieties we grow on the farm and feeling proud that when someone sticks their nose into my flowers, they inhale fragrance instead of chemicals. With each seed sown, weed pulled, and bridal bouquet created, I am building our future and living my dream. Following your dreams is never easy—it is hard work, sore muscles, fear of failure, loneliness, mistakes, and lots of dirty laundry. But having the courage to step out of my comfort zone and explore that restlessness, with the unfailing support of William, led me to start this flower business. It is the best risk I've ever taken. Now, years later and finally

farming our own land, I can say with certainty that the struggles and never-ending workdays were worth it. Growing flowers is what I was meant to do.

Flourishing

I read every book, blog post, and article I could find before starting my career as a flower farmer. I'm grateful for my background and that the actual growing has never been a challenge for me, but I never could find the right information on how to get started… I wanted the nitty gritty details. I gleaned a lot from vegetable farms and applied it to my flower-growing operation, and I learned a *lot* from trial and error. My hope is that this book will save you a few errors of your own.

Each parcel of land comes with its own strengths and challenges, and almost no one has the ideal growing conditions for creating a garden. Climate plays a huge role in gardening, and while it is possible to grow the same flowers in almost any climate, timing and seasonality vary greatly. I wanted to write a book with systems and principles that could work across a wide variety of locations and conditions—from tiny backyard gardens to flower farms on a few acres. The exact same systems and plans that we use at Flourish Flower Farm to grow high-quality, professional-grade flowers are laid out in this book for you. I hope to provide a flower-growing template that can be customized to help anyone grow a successful garden!

Flourish as a verb means "to grow or develop in a healthy or vigorous way, especially as the result of a particularly favorable environment." When we were deciding on a name for our farm, we wanted something simple and meaningful to our business and our lives. My mom came up with the idea of Flourish (she is a wealth of creative inspiration!), and we were hooked instantly. Flourish Flower Farm was created during a time of transition and deep personal longing for something more in our lives—we wanted to flourish as people and to do something heartfelt and important. Our goals are not only to provide a favorable environment for our plants to flourish, but also for everyone who is a part of Flourish Flower Farm to flourish and grow in a healthy way. My hope is that this book provides the inspiration and path for you to create a flourishing flower garden. Growing flowers brings so much joy and I cannot wait to help you get started!

Xo Niki

Chapter 1

Know Your Climate

When the dream of operating my own flower farm started to bloom, I was overwhelmed by how many different types of flowers I wanted to grow. My wish list was a mile long! Growing up in a family of horticulturalists, I already knew that some wouldn't grow well (and some wouldn't grow at all) in my particular climate. For example, many of the tropical plants I watched my dad grow as a landscaper in coastal South Carolina would not survive a winter outdoors in the Blue Ridge Mountains. Trust me, I've killed my fair share of plants by planting them at the wrong time of year. I've coveted the long-stemmed sweet peas that thrive in the long, cool spring weather of the Pacific Northwest and felt like a failure when I could not achieve those results here in North Carolina, where we often speed past spring and go straight into summer temperatures. In actuality, my "failure" to grow long-stemmed sweet peas has nothing to do with my skills as a grower—it has everything to do with my climate.

Deciphering plant jargon and nomenclature is one of the most confusing aspects of learning to garden. What is a hardiness zone? How do I even know what zone I am in? Does my zone even matter? Like many aspects of gardening, you can dive deep into the science and endlessly research the perfectly precise way of doing things. You can also learn some basic tenets to know enough to get your hands dirty and grow a very successful flower garden.

About Hardiness Zones

The US Department of Agriculture has divided the country into thirteen different zones, with each zone being ten degrees Fahrenheit warmer or colder than the average winter in the adjacent zone. The map of hardiness zones of Europe divides the continent into eleven zones, ranging from -50 degrees Celsius to 10 degrees Celsius. Australia and Canada also have their own respective hardiness zone maps.

Hardiness zones are based on the minimum extreme coldest temperature for each zone, and while they can be helpful for determining whether a perennial will survive in a certain area, they alone do not provide enough information for planning a garden. They are not very helpful to gardeners looking for what to plant when. Two geographical areas can technically be in the same hardiness zone, but have drastically different climates and seasons.

A Note About Perennials, Annuals, Hardy Annuals, and Bulbs

Perennials are plants that continue to grow year after year. They typically grow during the warm spring and summer months, then go dormant during the winter months. Perennials can be a larger financial investment initially, but many will grow for five to over a hundred years, becoming more robust and productive each year. Examples include peonies, garden roses, lilacs, hydrangeas, and hellebores.

Annuals, or tender annuals, are typically planted during the spring and summer months. They bloom for one season and then die with a frost or when daylight becomes shorter. Annuals are replanted by seed again the next year. Tender annuals are very sensitive to cold temperatures and prefer growing in warm conditions. Examples include sunflowers, zinnias, marigolds, celosias, and cosmos.

Hardy annuals, or biennials, are a group of plants that prefer to grow in cold temperatures to establish their roots. They are planted either in the fall months (in climates without a deep, extended winter freeze) or in the early spring, and will bloom that same spring and summer. Biennials then die back the winter after they have bloomed. Examples include snapdragons, corncockles, delphiniums, dianthus, and foxgloves.

Bulbs are perennial plants that have their own food source attached, meaning they live and flower for multiple years. Most flowering bulbs are planted in the late fall (before the ground freezes) and remain dormant throughout the winter. The bulbs will then send up shoots in the spring and produce foliage and flowers. Examples of bulbs are tulips, narcissi, muscari, fritillaries, and lilies.

Tubers and corms are other types of plants which we will discuss in more detail later. The most common flowers grown from tubers are dahlias; ranunculus and anemone are grown from corms.

Freezing Temperatures

Understanding when your area may experience freezing temperatures is perhaps the most important aspect of gardening. Freezing causes ice crystals to form inside the plant's cells, bursting the cells or severely damaging them. Bottom line: it causes the plant to die. This is why deciduous trees and most flowering perennials drop their leaves in the winter and stop the process of photosynthesis; they regrow new leaves the following spring as the temperatures warm up.

Tender annuals cannot survive freezing temperatures, so knowing when it's safe to plant them is extremely important. There is nothing more disheartening to a gardener than lovingly starting plants from seed, only to transplant into the garden too early and have them killed by a late frost. In the US, the Farmer's Almanac provides average annual frost dates by zip code, with the "last frost" being sometime in spring and the "first frost" occurring in the fall. Tender annuals should only be planted after this last frost date. Most biennials and flowering bulbs should be planted around the first frost date, before winter sets in and the ground freezes. Perennials are best planted in the fall or early spring, as they are less likely to be scorched or dehydrated by the summer heat.

Growing Climates

Comparing hardiness zones, frost dates, and directions on seed packets can leave a gardener confused. "What should I plant when?" is a question I am asked very frequently. In an effort to simplify planting times and provide a general reference, I've broken things down into three general growing climates. These climates are based on growing in a field or out in the open, not in a space with auxiliary heat such as a greenhouse.

The Three General Climates

Warm

Warm climates are areas where the ground never freezes and where temperatures rarely dip below freezing. Extremely hot temperatures (consistently over 85 degrees Fahrenheit/29 degrees Celsius) make growing flowers difficult during the summer months. Gardeners are otherwise able to grow almost year-round, with spring and fall being especially robust growing seasons. Many of my friends who garden in warm climates take summers off.

Mild

Mild climates are areas that experience all four seasons. The ground rarely freezes during the winter, and, when it does, it's usually only for short periods of time. Summer temperatures rarely top 85 degrees Fahrenheit/20 degrees Celsius. Gardeners in the northern hemisphere can grow from about March through late October.

Cool

Cool climates are areas that experience freezing temperatures over an extended period of time. The ground typically freezes over in the winter, making it difficult to plant anything in the fall except hardy bulbs. Most hardy annuals are best planted in early spring when the ground thaws.

Chapter 2

Choosing and Preparing a Garden Plot

Tools: *silage tarp, sandbags, rototiller, shovel, trowel or hori hori knife*

Choosing a place for your garden is also of utmost importance. Most of us have less than ideal circumstances for gardening, but there are some important considerations to keep in mind that will help your garden flourish. I have grown flowers in sandy soil at the beach, in heavy clay in the piedmont, in a flood plain in the mountains (where it flooded a lot!), and currently on a sloping hill. It is possible to grow flowers in almost any condition by getting your soil prepared properly.

Growing Organically

Growing our flower farm "organically" (I use quotations because we are not certified organic) was a priority from day one. William and I consider ourselves stewards of the land where we live and farm, and we hope to preserve its natural beauty for many generations. We do not use any chemicals, synthetic fertilizers, or sprays to control weeds or pests. Introducing these chemicals disrupts the existing natural balance and rhythms, and we love creating a haven for songbirds, toads, butterflies, and bees on our farm. Removing

perennial weeds and Japanese beetles by hand takes more time and grit than spraying, but we know that our soil and land become healthier each year, and our employees, customers, pets, and ourselves are not exposed to harmful chemicals. One must take the long view when growing sustainably and creating a space where nature can flourish is a gift that we cherish.

Laying Out a Garden Plot

Two crucial considerations when determining a location for your garden plot are sunlight and drainage.

Sunlight

Most annual flowers grow best in areas with at least six to eight hours of full sun. Notice the path of the sun in your proposed garden plot throughout the day and at different times of the year… Are there any trees or structures (like your house) that cast shadows and provide too much shade? It may look like an area receives full sun in the winter when the trees have dropped their leaves, but the plot may actually be shady in the summer. Do you have full morning sun, but then only an hour of afternoon sunlight? Observing the sun's path will help you narrow down your options for a successful, sunny garden plot.

Drainage

Choose a spot that does not have standing water after it rains. Avoid concave areas—you want the water to drain freely and not puddle near the roots of plants, which causes the roots to rot and encourages disease. Gardening on a hillside or gentle slope can be more challenging in some ways, but it allows water to move away from the plants freely. It is also possible to dig small ditches or trenches around the garden to divert water away during heavy rains.

Other Considerations

+ You will need to water your garden frequently, so choose a location that can be reached with a hose. Have a plan to make it as easy as possible to water the garden. More on irrigation in Chapter 7.

+ Air circulation is important for growing healthy plants. It's best to choose a plot away from dense trees and shrubs so that breezes can flow easily. Poor airflow leads to mildew and other diseases.

+ Know what is underground before you dig. Growing a garden on top of electrical, plumbing, or sewer lines can be dangerous and harmful. Call your local authorities to locate important utility lines.

Soil Preparation

There are probably a hundred different ways to prepare a garden plot, and choosing the right method largely depends on the tools available to you.

Silage Tarp

The method of soil preparation involving the least financial investment is tarping. Silage tarps are large black plastic tarps laid flat on the ground. Silage tarps kill weeds by occultation: the plastic creates a warm, humid environment to stimulate weed germination and blocks out light, thus killing the weeds. Use a tarp that is large enough to cover the entire garden plot and secure the edges with sandbags, bricks, or anything heavy placed on top. Be sure to secure it well, especially if you live in an area with high wind. The silage tarp on our farm becomes a giant sail when not secured with enough weight. Silage tarps will kill grass, lawn, and weeds if left out for long enough—six months in the winter and three to four months in the summer. After removing the tarp, the ground should be softer with no grass and just soil.

Rototilling

Tilling is a quick, efficient way to prepare garden beds. If you prefer to not invest in a tiller of your own, some home improvement stores and extension offices rent tillers by the day or week. Renting is a great option because most gardeners only need to use a tiller once or twice a year. The rotating tines on a tiller rip up grass and turn up soil, creating a smooth bed for planting. When breaking new ground, it often takes several passes to create a smooth bed. Begin with the tines in a shallow position to tear apart grass, and gradually move deeper to break up the soil. End with a shallow pass of the tiller to smooth out the bed. It is important to rototill only when the ground is dry, otherwise the soil will clump and may create a hard, compacted layer under the path of the tines. Tilling also churns up weed seeds, so be prepared for new weeds to germinate even if the bed initially looks weed-free.

At Flourish, our ideal soil preparation for new garden beds follows these steps:

1. Cover the new garden bed with a silage tarp for several months.

2. Rototill until the soil is smooth and loose.

3. Cover with the silage tarp again for several weeks to suffocate new weed growth.

4. Plant immediately after removing the silage tarp.

Raised Beds

Another option is to create raised garden beds instead of gardening directly in the ground. Raised beds (also known as garden boxes) are more of a financial investment up front, but have many benefits, including good drainage and less weed pressure. They are also aesthetically pleasing and require no tilling or tarping. DIY building plans and kits are readily available online. It's best to build with untreated wood, as treated wood leaches chemicals into the soil. Line the bottom of the raised bed with cardboard to create a barrier between your soil and the grass, killing grass and softening the soil more quickly. Fill the raised bed/garden box with high-quality topsoil.

No-Till or Lasagna Gardening

No-till is a method of growing that does not disturb the layers of the soil. One common term for no-till gardening is "lasagna gardening," because organic and biodegradable materials are layered on top of the undisturbed soil. No-till soil preparation requires more time initially than tilling but has many long-term benefits, such as reduced soil compaction and erosion. One common recipe for a no-till garden is as follows: spread corrugated cardboard on top of the soil (which essentially accomplishes the same results as a silage tarp), followed by three to four inches of compost or high-quality topsoil on top of the cardboard. Plants will be planted directly into the compost. The cardboard will decompose after a few weeks, allowing the plants' roots to reach the natural soil underneath once it has been softened by the cardboard.

Most of us do not garden with ideal circumstances or have access to a rototiller, but any of these methods will give you a great starting point for a garden.

All About Soil

Talking about soil can be intimidating—there is an entire field of scientific study called pedology related to soils. By understanding just a few basic concepts, you can know all that you need to without getting overwhelmed. Why do I use the word "soil" instead of "dirt"? Soil is alive, while dirt is dead. Soil is made of living organisms, bacteria, worms, minerals, air, moisture, and the decaying bodies and waste of living organisms. Dirt is what you get under your fingernails and on the knees of your pants after a day of working in the garden—it cannot support life, and your garden will not thrive in dirt alone.

Do I Have Dirt or Soil?

Testing the soil is the perfect way to understand what you're working with. Without knowing that the human body has a normal temperature of 98 degrees, it would be impossible to define what constitutes a fever; we need a baseline. A soil test gives you that baseline knowledge of how healthy your soil is and what you need to add to make it healthier. Soil tests are offered through each state's agricultural Cooperative Extension Service office. These offices work with a state's prominent university or the US Department of Agriculture, and soil testing is offered for a small fee (or for free!). Soil test kits are also available for purchase online through private laboratories. Soil testing needs to be completed by a laboratory—this is not something you can do at home. Taken from a sampling of your garden plot, soil tests provide a snapshot of your garden soil's health. Samples can be taken during any time of the year, but I recommend sampling during the winter months, giving you time to make adjustments as needed before the spring. Soil testing should be completed annually if you are aiming to make big adjustments, or every two to three years for more routine check-ups.

How to Take a Soil Sample

1. Remove the grass or rocks from a small area of your garden.

2. Use a trowel to take a "slice" of soil about eight inches deep and one inch wide.

3. Place into a plastic bag, bucket, or container. Using plastic is important because other containers can cause interference with the test results.

4. Repeat the slicing process in five to ten more areas of your garden, choosing spots in a zig-zag pattern. Mix all the soil slices together.

5. If you are having multiple garden beds tested, label the plastic containers with the name of the area.

6. Follow the instructions for sending the soil test to the testing facility.

What Will the Soil Test Tell Me?

The most important pieces of information you need to know from the soil test are (1) the pH of your soil and (2) the levels of available nutrients. Good soils are mostly neutral, with a pH of about 6.0–7.0. The lower the number, the more acidic the soil. The soil test may make recommendations on how to increase the pH and make it less acidic (confusing, I know) by adding a specific amount of lime (see the sidebar on adding lime). If you have very acidic soil, the microorganisms—all the good guys that live in the soil and help make your plants healthy—may be limited or nonexistent. If the soil pH is too alkaline, you can add acidic elements like pine bark or peat moss. Soil pH also affects the availability of nutrients, but that can get very complicated; what you really need to understand is that a balanced pH is good for gardening.

The soil test report will also give you recommendations on adding fertilizer based on the levels of available nutrients. The recommendations are largely based on measurements of phosphorous (P) and potassium (K). Even though nitrogen (N) is a crucial component of soil health, it is not typically measured in routine soil tests because it is quite mobile–the levels can vary widely at different times of the year. The recommendations section of the soil test will provide guidance for application of N-P-K fertilizer. "N-P-K" is printed on almost all bags of fertilizer and indicates the ratio of those elements in that particular fertilizer.

Calculating the Amount of Lime and Fertilizer to Apply

First, determine your square footage by multiplying the length of the area by the width of the area. For example, a thousand-square-foot area is fifty feet by twenty feet. Divide that number by a thousand to obtain the number of units to be treated. Multiplying the number of units by the pounds of material necessary to treat a thousand square feet will give you the amount of fertilizer and lime needed.

Example 1:

If the garden area is 500 feet by 20 feet, and the suggested lime or fertilizer treatment is 30M (pounds per 1,000 square feet):

500 feet × 20 feet = 10,000 square feet
Divide 10,000 square feet by 1,000 = 10 units
Multiply 30 pounds by 10 units = 300 pounds of material (fertilizer or lime)

Example 2:

If the garden area is 10 feet by 20 feet, and the suggested lime or fertilizer treatment is 30M (pounds per 1,000 square feet):

10 feet × 20 feet = 200 square feet
Divide 200 square feet by 1,000 = 0.20 units
Multiply 30 pounds by 0.20 units = 6 pounds of material (fertilizer or lime)

Adding Compost

Now that you understand the existing components of your soil, you can begin adding compost and other nutrients as needed. In general, adding organic matter is always a good idea, and here's an oversimplified version of why: there are millions of tiny organisms living in the soil that help make a healthy and live (not dead, like dirt) ecosystem. Healthy soil allows you to grow beautiful, healthy flowers. These tiny creatures living in the soil need to eat, and we can feed them by adding good things into the soil. These creatures like to eat compost, green manure, and cover crops (more on those later), legumes, animal manure, and organic mulch.

The best way to add organic matter before planting is to add compost. Most of us do not have access to homemade compost, and creating enough compost for a full garden plot is difficult to achieve without ample space and time. Buying bagged or bulk compost is a great solution. You can source compost from a local mulch yard or gardening store. Using finished or fully decomposed compost is of the utmost importance! Finished compost smells earthy and is dark brown and crumbly. Using unfinished compost, or compost that has not fully decomposed yet, will essentially make the nutrients (especially nitrogen) unavailable to your plants. The tiny organisms in the soil are eating those same nutrients to fuel themselves while they break down the partially decomposed parts of the compost.

For soil low in organic matter (which is unveiled in the soil test report), add two to three inches of finished compost to your garden plot. Ideally, you should lightly mix the compost into the existing soil with a rake, but leaving the compost as a top layer is also fine. For soils with ample organic matter, add one inch of compost. I recommend adding compost in the spring, just before planting, but there really is no wrong time to add it. Compost continues to decompose throughout the year, and the amount of organic matter in the soil will slowly decline, so adding compost every year is recommended, especially in hot climates. Heat makes everything decompose more quickly.

Gardens with soil that are amended with compost hold air and water better, drain more efficiently, contain nutrients for plants to use, and have fewer insect and disease problems. The compost also helps support more of those tiny beneficial organisms, which help control harmful organisms.

Chapter 3

Planning What to Plant

Tools: measuring tape or wheel, flags, garden notebook

Narrowing down what to plant in a cutting garden can be difficult if you're like me and want to plant ALL THE FLOWERS! Let's start with a plan for what actually fits in your garden plot and what will thrive in your climate. The goals of this book are to grow flowers in a cutting garden or small-scale flower farm, and to create beautiful arrangements, so we will focus on flower varieties and methods that accomplish those goals.

Measuring Your Garden Plot

While taking the steps to plan and prepare your garden plot (as described in this chapter), you can simultaneously measure your garden to begin planning what to plant. Order seeds, bulbs, and tools months in advance of planting to ensure that your favorite varieties do not sell out and that you have everything needed when the time comes to plant. Simplify garden planning by making all the garden beds the same length and width (though this is not something we're able to do at Flourish because we are limited by our hilly terrain). You can also simplify planning by planting almost all flowers nine or twelve inches apart. If you purchase annual plants from a garden center, the information provided with the plant will likely indicate different (further apart) spacing, which is geared toward landscaping versus a cutting garden. Tighter spacing

encourages plants to grow taller with longer stems and is suitable for almost all varieties of annual and hardy annual flowers.

How to Plan a Garden with 4-Foot Beds and 2.5-Foot Pathways Like We Do at Flourish

+ Begin by measuring the length and width of your plot. Stake the top two corners with flags.

+ Lay measuring tape along the top of your field and place flags every 4 feet for the beds, followed by every 2.5 feet for the pathways.

+ Count the total number of beds.

+ Multiply the length of one bed by the total number of beds. This gives you the total area of available planting space.

+ Spacing plants nine inches apart will fit approximately 9 plants per 1 linear foot per 4-foot wide bed.

+ Multiply the total area of planting space by 9 to give you the total number of plants you can have in the ground at one time.

Note: The same principles can be used with your garden, even if it's a different configuration.

Now that you know the total number of plants that you can grow in your entire garden space, it's time to decide what to plant. I plan my garden by starting with three lists: hardy annuals, tender annuals, and others (tubers, bulbs, etc.). These groups of flowers will be planted at different times throughout the year, but the principles for planning are the same. You'll just adjust the dates to best suit your climate.

Because of the scale on which I operate my flower farm, I plan with a spreadsheet. Good old pen and paper work too, and I highly recommend keeping a notebook devoted solely to your flower garden as well.

SAMPLE CROP PLANNING SPREADSHEET

Flower Type	Specific variety or color	Total # plants per planting	Date seeded indoors	Date transplanted into the garden	Date of first harvest	Date of last harvest
Snapdragon	Madame Butterfly Rose	128	Sept 7 January 4	October 26 March 1	January 4 April 15	 July 25
Agrostemma	Purple Queen	128	Sept 7 January 4 February 22	October 26 March 1 April 5	April 10	July 10
Cosmos	cupcakes white	72	March 23 April 13 May 4	May 4 May 25 June 15	June 1	October 20
Zinnia	Oklahoma Salmon	72	March 23 April 13 May 4	May 4 May 25 June 15	June 15	October 20

Crop Planning

The crop planning chart may seem like a lot of extra work up front, but I promise that it's worth the time to get organized with a clear system from the get-go. This information can be used every year, with slight adjustments as you learn and grow.

+ Begin by filling out the crop and variety cells with the approximate number of plants to sow with each planting.

+ Multiply that number by the number of times you plan on planting something (see the section on succession planting later in the chapter). For example, I plant Zinnia Oklahoma Salmon three times in a season, and each time I sow 72 seeds, which equals a total of 216 plants for the season.

+ Once you have entered every single flower variety that you want to plant, sum everything up in the "total number plants per season" column.

+ Compare the grand total from the spreadsheet to the total number of available spaces from measuring your garden plot before. Do you have more space available to plant? If so, yay! Add a few more flowers from the wish list to the spreadsheet. If you don't have enough space, it's time to begin prioritizing and culling.

+ A conservative estimate is to plant one-eighth to one-fourth more than the total number of available spaces. When the first planting of early season flowers stops blooming and can be removed from the garden, that space in the garden beds becomes available for a late season succession of summer annuals. It's a bit of an imperfect puzzle, but growing and blooming times will vary from year to year depending on the weather. Just go with it and try not to stress too much.

+ Another option is to have enough space in the garden beds available for an entire season's worth of flowers, making the garden less of a puzzle. The downside is that you have more overall space to prepare, weed, and maintain. I much prefer having a smaller overall space to tend, even if that means some plants are planted a week later than I originally anticipated while I wait for space to become available.

Keeping a Garden Journal

Keeping track of the first and last harvests helps tremendously with garden planning in upcoming years. I jot down little notes, such as, "The first few stems of anemone are short, but they grow longer the more I cut them." Other things that are helpful to keep track of are:

+ Extreme weather events or temperature swings

+ Number of days it takes for a particular variety of seed to germinate

+ Length of time from planting to blooming

+ Harvest amounts

+ Time spent on tasks like planting, weeding, staking/supporting, or harvesting

+ Does a specific variety of flower bloom abundantly? Or was it puny?

+ Is this variety a must-grow-again or not worth it?

Buying Seedlings Instead of Starting Flowers from Seed

If the thought of starting plants from seed is intimidating, you can often buy seedlings (a.k.a., baby flower plants) locally. It is best to buy seedlings from a reputable garden center instead of a big box store. Here are a few things to keep in mind as you shop for seedlings:

+ Many flowers from big box stores are treated with a growth regulator, which causes them to bloom on very short stems. Short stems are not ideal for cut flowers! Be sure to ask what the seedlings have been treated with before purchasing if you are unsure.

+ Never buy annual flower plants that are already blooming for your cutting garden. These plants are at a mature stage and will not continue to bloom for much longer, nor will they grow longer stems. Plants that are already blooming look great in containers if you're craving something instantly pretty.

+ Look for seedlings in trays or pots that are a maximum of three inches by three inches in size.

+ Seek out local flower farmers and ask if they offer flower seedlings for sale.

Days to Maturity

Listed on each seed packet are "Days to Maturity," or the number of days it takes for a plant to be ready to harvest (a.k.a., to be picked). This gives an estimate or range that lets you know how much growth time a plant requires before it blooms. I primarily measure in weeks or months, as the length of time will vary greatly depending on the weather, and weeks are way easier to keep track of than days. Begin counting the weeks after a plant is transplanted into the garden, not when the seed is started indoors. I have found that *most* seeds require about six to eight weeks of growing in the trays before they are ready to be transplanted into the outdoor garden (more on seed starting in Chapter 6). If you skip seed starting and transplant seedlings directly into the garden, the length of time before you're able to pick flowers varies depending on the specific flower variety and the weather. Is it sunny or overcast? Raining every day or not at all? Unseasonably cool for late spring or scorching hot? All of these factors will determine how long it will take the plants to reach maturity. Some flowers, such as cosmos, can bloom one month after transplanting, while others, like lisianthus, bloom four months after transplanting.

Checking the "days to maturity" of a plant will also allow you to count backward from the first frost date and plan when to plant a final succession. We want to allow the flower plenty of time to grow and bloom before the frost arrives. For example, a zinnia takes sixty to eighty days to mature, and I know from experience that it will bloom for at least 1.5 months (usually longer, but I feel that 1.5 months of bloom time would justify planting another succession). So I look at the calendar and count backward: our average first frost at Flourish is around October 23, and the zinnias need 2 months for maturity and 1.5 months for blooming. This puts my transplant date (a.k.a., the date I put the baby plants into the garden outside) at around mid-June. This is also great information to have handy in case you have unexpected available space in the garden and have time to plant something quick, like some sunflower varieties.

Plant Hardiness

Understanding the hardiness of each flower in your crop plan will help you know when to start your seeds. Seed packets provide this information, but it is not explicitly stated. Clues like "sow after the last frost" let you know a plant is not cold hardy at all. "Sow eight to ten weeks before the last frost" or "as soon as the soil can be worked" mean that those plants can handle some colder temperatures. Areas with warm climates never even experience a frost, so knowing what to plant when can be even more confusing.

WHEN TO PLANT OUTDOORS

Tender Annuals	Warm Climate	Mild Climate	Cold Climate
Ageratum	late winter	after last frost	after last frost
Amaranthus	late winter	after last frost	after last frost
Celosia	late winter	after last frost	after last frost
Cosmos	late winter	after last frost	after last frost
Dahlia	early spring or late summer	after last frost	after last frost
Dahlia	late winter	after last frost	after last frost
Lemon Basil	late winter	after last frost	after last frost
Lisianthus	late winter	early spring	early spring
Marigolds	late winter	after last frost	after last frost
Nicotiana	late winter	after last frost	after last frost
Phlox	autumn/winter	early spring	after last frost
Scabiosa	autumn/winter	autumn/winter/ early spring	early spring
Sunflower	late winter	after last frost	after last frost
Zinnia	late winter	after last frost	after last frost

Hardy Annuals	Warm Climate	Mild Climate	Cold Climate
Anemone	autumn	late autumn/early winter	late winter/ early spring
Bupleurum	autumn	autumn	early spring
Campanula	autumn	autumn	early spring
Corncockle	autumn	autumn/winter/early spring	early spring
Delphinium	autumn	autumn	early spring
Foxglove	autumn	autumn	early spring
Larkspur	autumn	autumn	early spring
Nigella	late autumn	autumn	early spring
Orlaya	autumn	autumn	early spring
Poppies	autumn	early spring	early spring
Ranunculus	autumn	late autumn/early winter	late winter/ early spring
Rudbeckia	autumn	autumn	early spring
Snapdragons	autumn	late autumn/early spring	early spring

Repeat Bloomers and One-Stem Bloomers

Maximizing real estate on my farm is a huge priority—I'm always aiming for the most flower abundance for my efforts. While each flower variety is unique, I put them into two general categories when it comes to the number of flowers per plant: repeat bloomers and one-stem bloomers. Like the name implies, repeat bloomers put out multiple stems and flowers per plant. They often bloom for months on end and the more you cut or harvest them, the more flowers they produce. One-stem bloomers, on the other hand, produce just one stem of flowers per plant. Because my goal is to grow more flowers as efficiently as possible, most of my space is dedicated to repeat bloomers. There are some flower varieties I consider to be one-stem bloomers that either grow multiple stems per plant or continue to bloom after the first big harvest, but the new growth is puny in comparison to the first cut. Whether it be stem length or the number of blooms per stem, it's not worth the space and maintenance on my farm to treat them as repeat bloomers. For backyard gardeners, flower abundance—even if smaller than the initial bloom—is a lovely bonus.

Favorite Repeat Bloomers

Zinnia, Cosmos, Poppy, Gomphrena, Queen Anne's Lace, Snapdragon, Ranunculus, Anemone, Foxglove, Forget-Me-Not, Feverfew, Delphinium, Dahlia, Celosia (spike varieties), Ageratum, Dianthus, Scabiosa, Sweet Pea, Phlox

Favorite One-Stem Bloomers

Bupleurum, Nigella, Sunflower, Stock, Celosia (cockscomb), Tulip, Lisianthus, Amaranthus

Succession Planting

Succession planting is when you plant the same crop multiple times throughout the season, staggering the times at which you plant. Succession planting has many benefits:

+ It allows you to enjoy a larger variety of flowers for a longer period of time.

+ By the time an early succession is not producing as many flowers (plants get tired, too), another succession should become available.

+ It curbs stress about difficult-to-manage summer diseases. Instead of treating unhealthy mature plants, infected plants can be removed from the garden and a new succession will be healthy and ready to bloom. Many summer diseases, such as powdery mildew, have spores that are spread by the wind. Once the infected plants are removed (and burned instead of added to a compost pile), the soil does not need to be treated before planting in the same place again. However, it is a good idea to rotate disease-prone flowers, like zinnias, and to only plant the same variety of flower in the same exact garden row every three years.

+ You can plant a smaller quantity of plants several times throughout the season, which leads to less deadheading and more robust plants.

Summer annuals can be succession planted three to five times throughout a season in warm and mild climates. Cool climates may only have enough frost-free days for one to two successions. Spacing each succession about three to four weeks apart is important, so you don't end up with too many of the same flowers blooming at once. In my first year as a professional flower farmer, I had over two thousand snapdragons bloom at the exact same time—I could hardly give them away fast enough!

Hardy annuals can be succession planted in warm and mild climates by planting one succession in the fall and one in late winter. The "Days to Maturity" counting backward calculations come in very handy when determining how many successions you can plant in a season.

Keeping good notes in your garden journal is especially important when it comes to tracking the planting and blooming times of succession planting. Although the weather changes from year to year, often changing your best laid plans, the information will be helpful when it comes time to plan next year's garden.

Planting for a Balanced Garden Bouquet

Another consideration when planning a flower garden is what you'll do with all of those beautiful flowers when they start blooming. Regular harvesting is important to keep plants steadily blooming (more on harvesting later), and putting thought into growing flowers that make for balanced arrangements is important. The joy of growing flowers comes from sharing your garden-fresh bouquets with others and, of course, enjoying them in your own home.

Even after many years of growing bouquets for markets and designing wedding flowers, I still have to be careful and make sure I have the proper mix of flowers blooming during each month to make balanced arrangements.

1. Focal flowers: lily, dahlia, sunflower, peony, garden rose, tulip

2. Greenery: lemon basil, eucalyptus, viburnum, sedum, baptisia, pittosporum, shiso

3. Filler: gomphrena, feverfew, statice, ageratum, forget-me-not, dianthus, ammi

4. Spikes: snapdragon, celosia, campanula, delphinium, larkspur, stock

5. Round: zinnia, rudbeckia, marigold, ranunculus, anemone, daffodil

6. Whimsy: scabiosa, nigella, cosmos, sweet pea on the vine, blackberry lily, amaranth

Ordering Seeds and Bulbs

Now that you have completed your crop spreadsheet, it's time to shop for seeds and bulbs! Like I mentioned before, ordering early is important because many varieties sell out quickly. I do my crop planning for spring and summer flowers in November/December and for fall-planted flowers in May/June. By this time, I have a good idea of how that season's flowers performed, and I generally have enough information to make decisions for the next season. Do I want to plant the same thing again next year? Was there too much to harvest, and should I plant less? Do I wish that I grew more of one flower and less of another? All these notes are kept in my garden journal. Plus, I always have a running list of flowers I saw someone else growing that I want to incorporate into my garden next season.

When it's time to go seed and bulb shopping, definitely have your spreadsheet handy. Trust me, the temptation to veer from the list is strong (so many pretty flowers and you'll want to grow them all!). I always end up with things that weren't on my list, and that I sadly have no extra room for in the garden.

If you plan to start growing your flower garden from seeds, total up the amount you plan to plant for each variety and add an extra 25 percent to that number. This is the approximate number of seeds to order. For example, if I plan to grow a total of 216 Zinnia Oklahoma Salmon plants throughout the season, I order at least 275 to 300 seeds. I always round up depending on the number of seeds per packet. Things happen—I accidentally drop two or five extra seeds in a cell, some don't germinate, or I spill them on the floor. It's nice to have extra, just in case.

For flower bulbs, I order very close to the exact number of bulbs that I wish to plant. Bulbs generally sprout more reliably than seedlings—there is less room for human error and fewer steps in the overall planting process—so you don't need to factor in as many extra. Ordering 5 to 10 percent more bulbs than you expect to grow is fine, or just round up to the next amount available per package.

Storing Seeds and Bulbs

Seeds should be stored in an airtight container out of heat, humidity, and direct sunlight. I store my seeds in an alphabetized accordion folder in the closet. Some seeds will be viable for several years if stored this way, but it's generally a good idea to buy fresh seeds every year for better success with germination.

Bulbs should only be stored for a short period of time—a few weeks or months—in a cool, dark place. Flower bulbs are shipped in early fall and are eager to sprout when they arrive. Keeping them in a cool, dark place tricks them into staying dormant until you're ready to plant them in the soil. Good airflow is important to prevent mold and fungus. I've had bulbs rot in my basement, and not only is it such a depressing waste of money, but it's also gross and smelly. Some cool weather bulbs, like daffodils and tulips, can be stored in a refrigerator until it's time to plant. Because bulbs are so prone to rotting, they must be stored dry in ventilated bags with wood shavings, dry peat moss, or vermiculite. They should also be kept away from fruits, as fruits emit a gas called ethylene. This gas causes fruits to ripen and causes problems with flower bulbs.

Chapter 4

Seed Starting and Planting

> **Tools:** *butter knife, seeding tool, plug tray, watering can,*
> *plant label tags for field and trays, garden marker, bulb trowel*

Now we're finally getting to the fun part: growing flowers! Planning and preparation are important in providing a good foundation for the flower garden. They also build anticipation for actually getting your hands dirty. Now that your crop plan is complete, you can follow the schedule you created to know when to start each kind of seed. I typically sow seeds on one day of the week and do a whole batch at once. It's nice to only get my seed starting materials out one time each week and really get in the zone. Plus, I only have one mess to clean up.

Seed starting and planting has a reputation for being complicated and tricky, but the truth is that plants want to grow! Seeds want to germinate and grow into flowers. It's up to us to provide the right conditions, then nature will do what it's meant to do. There are many ways to grow flowers and start seeds, and in general, there are very few "wrong" ways to go about it. (Truly, the only wrong way is the one that ends up killing the seedling before it has a chance to thrive.) I'm sharing my low-budget, uncomplicated approach to seed starting and planting—you can do it, too!

Creating an Indoor Grow Station

We do not have a greenhouse at Flourish, so we start all seeds using racks and LED lights in the flower studio (which is actually my garage). This system can be set up in a guestroom, bathtub, garage—anywhere with a regulated temperature and good airflow. The ideal temperature range is 55–70 degrees Fahrenheit/13–21 degrees Celsius. Using this system, I can have sixteen trays—over two thousand seedlings—growing at one time. Additional natural light is not needed, though it doesn't hurt. All of the necessary materials can be sourced from a local hardware store.

Grow Station Materials

+ Metal shelving racks.

+ LED shop lights, 4 feet long with 4 bulbs and 80 watts. I love using LED lights because they don't radiate heat, allowing the trays to maintain a more consistent moisture level. They're also more budget friendly than special grow lights. I have seen no difference in the quality of the seedlings that I grow under these lights versus ones under fancy bulbs.

+ (1) Power strip.

+ (1) Mechanical twenty-four-hour timer.

+ (1) Extension cord.

+ One-foot, double-loop chains (the number will depend on the number of metal shelving racks you are using).

+ Small S-hooks (the number will depend on the number of metal shelving racks you are using).

Seed Starting Materials

✦ Plug trays with 72 or 128 cells. High-quality trays made of heavy-duty plastic can be reused for many years.

✦ Open flats without holes. Double-check the measurements to ensure the plug trays fit inside these.

✦ Humidity dome, if you live in a place with low humidity. Maintaining airflow is important, otherwise the seedlings can dampen off (a.k.a., rot at the root). We don't need to use them at Flourish since we have ample humidity in our climate.

✦ Six-inch plant labels or bedding labels. I cut them in half because I'm thrifty. Used mini-blinds or popsicle sticks work great too.

✦ Garden marker pen.

✦ Seed starting soil mix, such as ProMix or Baccto Professional Planting Mix. A good seed starting mix is mostly made of peat moss, with some coarse perlite and balanced trace elements.

✦ Watering can.

✦ A note about heat mats: We no longer use heat mats at Flourish. I used them for many years and always found them to be a pain— the soil in our trays dried out unevenly, and keeping an eye on the temperature was one more task to do. I stopped using them and have had no change in the germination rate. We consistently have almost 100 percent germination. It is a step that I've happily eliminated from our seed starting process.

Growing and Caring for Seedlings

+ Fill the plug trays with soil, making sure every single cell is full and that the soil is mildly compacted. If the soil isn't compacted enough, the roots will not become as strong and may dampen off. If it's compacted too much, the little roots have to work too hard to grow strong.

+ Water the plug trays well with a watering can. I make sure the soil is very damp (but not soggy) before I start seeding, so I don't have to water immediately after putting the seeds in the trays. I just water overhead gently with a watering can.

+ Use your fingertips to make a tiny divot in each cell. This gives the seed a place to rest.

+ Create a label with the name of the variety and place it in a corner of the tray.

+ Place one seed per cell.

+ After the tray is full of seeds, sprinkle vermiculite or more seed starting mix on top. Gently smooth it over so the seed is covered with about a quarter-inch of soil.

+ Place the seeded trays on your racks. Using the chains, position the lights about one to two inches above the top of the tray. You want the lights to remain as close as possible to the plants for the entire time that they're growing. If the lights are too far away, the plants will "get leggy," or reach and stretch toward the lights. As the plants grow, use the chains and S-hooks to raise the height of the lights.

✦ Use the mechanical timer to automatically turn the lights on and off. The lights should be on for about fourteen hours per day, with most of those hours being during the daytime.

✦ About watering: I tend to let my trays get a little dry (without being too dry and zapping the seedlings) before watering. Erring on the side of a tiny bit dry is much better than overwatering. Overwatering will cause them to dampen off. When the soil changes to a lighter brown, that's when I water.

Transplanting into the Garden

Germinating is when a seed sends a tiny sprout up through the soil. Some plants will germinate within a couple of days, some will take over a week. Just be patient and don't overwater. The first leaves to grow, called cotyledon, are baby leaves (kind of like baby teeth). The cotyledon drop off after they have served their purpose of giving energy to the tiny new plant. The next set of leaves to grow are called the "true leaves." These will stay with the plant throughout its entire life cycle. When a seedling has two to three sets of true leaves and is three to four inches (eight to ten centimeters) tall, it's almost ready to transplant outside.

Hardening Off

Hardening off is the process of gently acclimatizing the seedling to a noncontrolled environment—a.k.a., the great outdoors. The seedling has been happily growing in perfectly controlled conditions for its entire life thus far; going from those perfect conditions to the harsh outdoor world can be very traumatic. By hardening off seedlings, we gradually get them used to things like real sunshine, wind, and rain.

Move the trays of seedlings into a sheltered spot outdoors for a few hours on the first day. Gradually increase the number of hours they are outdoors each day, paying special attention to heavy rain and wind. Again, we're trying to ease them into the real world. After about a week, the seedlings are ready to be planted into the garden beds. Sometimes I have to wait longer depending on the weather—a cold snap in the spring, excessive rain, very hot temperatures, or no rain in the forecast.

Transplanting

Transplanting is simply moving a plant from one location to another. In this case, we're moving the seedlings from their plug trays into the garden beds. The garden should be prepared and ready to go (as outlined in Chapter 3) before you're ready to transplant, otherwise the seedlings may remain in their trays too long and become rootbound.

My favorite tool for transplanting is a butter knife. Using the butter knife, gently guide the seedling out of the plug tray. I like to take out five to ten seedlings in a row and lay them on the ground. Then, use the butter knife to open up a small hole in the soil. Use your fingers to gently press around the seedling so there is good contact between the seedling and the soil. Keep moving along until the tray is empty.

You don't want to plant in the heat of the day because delicate seedlings can dry out very quickly. We usually plant in the morning or late afternoon at Flourish. Give them a good drink of water immediately after planting and keep them watered well for the first couple of days if there is no rain. We'll talk more about irrigation in Chapter 6.

Planting Bulbs

Planting bulbs like daffodils, tulips, fritillaria, and muscari is not as complicated or time-consuming as planting seedlings. Flower bulbs should be planted in the fall, when the bulbs are dormant. Environmental conditions like soil temperature and moisture will trigger the bulbs to wake up and start growing.

In colder climates where the ground freezes during the winter, it is important to plant bulbs while you can still work the soil. The cold winter temperatures in these climates will provide the necessary vernalization (or winter cooling) for tulips and narcissi to grow on long stems. These flowers need a long period, about twelve weeks, of vernalization in order to flower and grow properly. Vernalization occurs naturally in cold climates and can be achieved artificially in warmer climates. Tulips and narcissi should be planted in the late fall in cooler climates where the ground freezes.

For warm or mild climates where the ground does not freeze (or only does for a short period of time), tulip and narcissus bulbs should be planted in December or January. The bulbs can be cooled in a refrigerator for up to four months before planting, creating an artificial vernalization period. Do not store bulbs in plastic in the fridge because they require ventilation—paper bags, egg cartons, mesh, or canvas bags are best. And do not store bulbs with fruit, as fruit emits ethylene gas which will ruin the bulbs. Storing bulbs in the fridge for about six to eight weeks before planting is ideal. Only take the bulbs out of the fridge when you are ready to plant.

For planting thirty bulbs or less at one time, a bulb trowel works great. My favorite method of planting a large quantity of bulbs is the trench method.

+ Begin by staking four corners of the area you plan to plant with flags, so you know where to dig.

+ Using a shovel, dig out a rectangle that is about three to four feet wide and eight to twelve inches deep. Shovel the soil that you dig onto the side of the trench.

+ A general rule of thumb is to plant a bulb three times as deep as its height.

+ Place the bulbs like eggs in a carton, typically with the pointy side up.

+ Cover the bulbs with the soil you removed earlier.

+ Think about what a great workout you just had!

+ Only water the bulbs if you experience many weeks without rain. Most bulbs are prone to rot and do not require supplemental watering aside from rainfall.

Deep Dive: Growing Dahlias

+ Prepare the garden bed in full sun (at least eight hours per day) with well-draining soil. If summer temperatures are extreme (for example, consistently over 90 degrees Fahrenheit), they may benefit from slight afternoon shade. For mild and cool climates, plant dahlias after all danger of frost has passed. For warm climates, plant dahlias in September and/or February to avoid growing during the hottest summer months.

+ Dig a trench or hole about six to eight inches deep and add a sprinkle of organic compost or fertilizer. We use a well-balanced 5-5-5 organic fertilizer at Flourish.

+ Dahlia tubers should be spaced eighteen to twenty-four inches apart. Ample spacing to allow good airflow is important, as dahlias are prone to powdery mildew, especially in warm, humid climates. Lay the tuber horizontally, sprout-side up. Cover the tuber so it's buried with about three inches of soil.

+ Do not water dahlias until they begin sprouting because the tubers are very prone to rotting.

+ Dahlias need to be kept weed-free until they are mature, since most weeds grow rapidly and can outcompete the dahlias for sunlight and soil nutrition. Plus, some weeds attract harmful pests. Ideally, dahlias are always kept weed-free (but I know how that goes!) and once they mature, they are large enough to win out over the weeds. Use organic mulch, such as wheat, straw, or cardboard around the plants to prevent weeds and conserve moisture.

+ When the plants are about twelve inches tall and have at least four sets of leaves, pinch back the main stem by snipping off about four inches of the growth center or central growing stem. This encourages good branching, giving you more stems and blooms in the long run.

+ After the plants are established and are about twelve inches tall, water them deeply once or twice per week (more watering is recommended for temperatures over 85 degrees). Drip irrigation or soaker hoses for watering are strongly recommended to help with disease control. More about the benefits of drip irrigation in Chapter 6.

✦ Dahlias need a support structure to keep the heavy blooms from bending to the ground. Tomato cages work great for small amounts of plants. For long rows of dahlias, horizontal Tenax netting or staking using a corral or the "Florida Weave" (both using T-posts and bailing twine) are recommended. More about plant support in Chapter 6.

✦ The more you cut your dahlias, the more they keep blooming! We cut our stems about every three days, even if it's just deadheading. This encourages the plant to keep producing flowers, versus going to seed. Cut deeply on long stems to continue promoting longer stem growth. Cut when the flowers are most of the way open (about three-quarters or so). Dahlia flowers do not open much more once they've been cut. Check the back of the plant for firm petals; browning or thin petals mean the bloom has matured and will not last as long in a vase.

Deep Dive: Growing Ranunculus and Anemone

Ranunculus and anemone are some of the most coveted spring flowers for good reason. Ranunculus may perhaps be my favorite flower of all time (shhh, don't tell the others), so I have perfected my system of growing these beauties over the years. These flowers can be grown in almost any climate and the system for growing both ranunculus and anemone is basically the same, though the timing of when to start the pre-sprouting and planting processes differs depending on your climate. Ranunculus and anemone are both grown from corms. Corms are similar to bulbs, but are small underground plant stems that act as food storage structures for certain plants. In my opinion, they look like shrived up sea creatures.

When to plant:

+ Warm climates in November.

+ Mild climates from October through late January.

+ Cool climates from January (if planted in a hoop house) through March (if planted outdoors).

General Growing Information

Here in western North Carolina where our winter temperatures frequently dip below freezing, I prefer to plant ranunculus and anemone in a hoop house (a small, unheated greenhouse-like structure) to have a little more control over the environment. But they don't need to be planted in a hoop house! For mild and cool climates, planting them under layers of light-filtering frost cloth works well too (you want to let the light in, not keep it out). You'll want to adjust your planting time according to the location of where you will plant—hoop house or field. If you have a hoop house, you can plant earlier in the winter because the plants will have more protection from freezing temperatures throughout the winter. If you plant in a field/garden, it's best to plant later in the winter so there are less drastic and frequent temperature fluctuations. If you are in a warm climate, planting in the late autumn is ideal to provide the most amount of growth time during the cooler winter months.

I tend to leave the end walls of our hoop house open for the duration of winter. Ranunculus and anemone are prone to root rot and fungal diseases, so they require good air movement and drainage. If the temperatures dip below 20 degrees Fahrenheit/-6 degrees Celsius, I close the end walls of the hoop house and cover the plants with a layer of frost cloth. I uncover in the morning as soon as it starts to warm up.

Once the soil is dry enough, I go through the bed with the walk-behind tiller. I start first with a shallow till, then do a deeper pass, and finish with a light till to smooth the bed. After tilling, I lay down reusable woven landscape fabric in the pathways so that there is no weeding or maintenance required. I do not plant ranunculus or anemone directly into landscape fabric, as the added heat is not good for these particular flowers (more on using landscape fabric in Chapter 6). After tilling and laying fabric in the pathways, I spread organic compost and fertilizer in each bed and mix them into the soil with a rake.

Pre-Sprouting

About ten to fourteen days before I'm ready to plant in the soil, I soak and pre-sprout the corms. I usually prepare the planting beds after I've started this process. There are many different ways to pre-sprout your corms, but I have had success by keeping it simple. Because ranunculus and anemone are prone to bacterial issues and our climate receives lots of rainfall in the winter, I soak my corms in an organic bacterial fungicide solution. Bacterial fungicide is a concentrated, beneficial microorganism that establishes itself on plant roots, and it can be purchased from most home gardening shops or online. (I also use it to drench all lisianthus plugs before planting and have eliminated fungal issues.) Even though I shy away from using any chemicals, this product is approved for certified organic production and helps protect my large investment in the corms. Root Shield and Actinovate are two brands that I recommend.

I soak corms until they start to plump up and double in size—about twelve hours for ranunculus and eight hours for anemone. After soaking, I fill large seed starting trays (the bottom trays without holes) with seed starting soil. I "plant" each corm into the tray so that the legs are facing down and the corms are touching, but not overlapping. I then cover them with a light dusting of the same seed starting soil or vermiculite.

My basement is the perfect spot for pre-sprouting, as it's about 60 degrees Fahrenheit/15 degrees Celsius, with medium humidity and minimal light. I check the corms every few days to make sure the soil is slightly moist, but not damp (err on the side of too dry rather than too wet). After about ten days, the corms grow little white rootlets and they're ready to go. Oftentimes, I am so busy during this time that by the time I get around to planting, they have half-inch white sprouts growing. No need to worry, they continue growing in the soil just fine.

Planting

Although I grow almost everything at the farm in landscape fabric, I do not plant ranunculus or anemone into fabric. I've found that the leaves and blooms of anemone get stuck under the fabric, and the ranunculus do not appreciate the extra heat and moisture retention caused by the fabric. Also, I have more time in the winter and early spring for a few rounds of weeding before the plants mature.

I typically plant four rows per bed of ranunculus and five of anemone, with six-inch spacing. I made a super high-tech planting spacer out of a conduit pole and flagging tape. One person uses the spacer to lay the sprouted corms along the rows and another person follows behind, planting them about one to two inches deep. My favorite planting tool is also super fancy: a butter knife from Goodwill. It's amazing how quickly you can plant a few thousand plants using this method!

Depending on how damp the soil already is, I may give it a light spray of water after planting. If I'm planting in a hoop house, I run lines of drip irrigation for occasional watering over the winter, and I only water when the temperatures will be above freezing the following day and night (you want to avoid freezing the roots). I water more frequently in the spring. Ranunculus and anemone grow quickly and don't require much maintenance throughout the winter, except occasional weeding and protection from those super chilly nights.

Chapter 5

Tending the Garden

Tools: *stirrup hoe, hori hori knife, knee pads*

Believe it or not, the most complicated aspect of gardening still lies ahead: plant care and maintenance. Now that your seedlings have been transplanted into the garden, they require diligent care to help them grow into healthy, mature plants. But don't be discouraged—all you need is a good plan for watering, weeding, and staking/support. Surprisingly, maintenance can be one of the most joyful aspects of gardening. I like to think that I'm nurturing my plants instead of maintaining them.

Weeding

Weeds are my second least favorite aspect of gardening (pests are definitely my least favorite), but the good thing is that they can be controlled organically with a little elbow grease. Even the most diligent gardeners end up having a weedy garden at some point—we have an herb garden at Flourish that we jokingly refer to as the "weed garden" because of the sheer number of weeds growing. It can be so frustrating when weeds seem to grow exponentially overnight, and the garden plants seem to grow at a snail's pace. By removing the weeds from the garden beds, we give the seedlings more space for their roots to spread, better airflow, and less competition for nutrients in the soil. It is actually true that many weeds grow more quickly than transplants because

the weeds have a head start—their roots are already established. The main idea behind weeding is to stay ahead of the game by removing weeds before they can outcompete and overshadow your seedlings and never letting weeds go to seed.

Here Are a Few Ways to Help Control Weeds

Landscape Fabric

At Flourish, we actually grow almost all of our plants in landscape fabric. The landscape fabric has a perfect pattern for planting: holes two inches in diameter, spaced nine or twelve inches apart. Because we're growing thousands upon thousands of plants at any given time, the weeds and grass would grow *way* quicker than we could ever keep up with. Landscape fabric essentially works the same way as a silage tarp: it kills everything under the black fabric and the seedlings are planted into the two-inch holes. The bases of most annual flowers are small enough that two inches is the perfect amount of space for the seedling to grow, and generally only one round of weeding is needed before the plant grows large enough to outcompete any weeds. Landscape fabric is laid over a prepared garden bed (before planting) and secured to the ground with landscape sod staples. Using landscape fabric is an excellent way to manage weeds organically. Although the fabric is a financial investment up front, it pays for itself many times over with the labor saved from not having to weed as much, plus it lasts for eight to ten or more years. The downside to landscape fabric is that it is a bit of an eyesore, especially when the seedlings are still tiny—it can look like a sea of black fabric in your yard.

Straw Mulch

Using an organic mulch material, such as straw, is another method of controlling weeds. Straw mulch holds in moisture and suffocates many weeds before they can sprout. We use straw mulch on our dahlias, which have a large base at the bottom of the plant, and on our perennials, which spread and grow larger over time. We use landscape fabric to define the pathways between garden beds, so that the pathways themselves do not require weeding or mowing, and lay straw in the main garden bed around the plants. One downside to straw is that it's never 100 percent free of weed seeds, so there is inevitable weeding to be done. Mulch also needs to be applied at least once a season, if not more often. Straw should be applied at a depth of two to three inches for maximum benefit.

Hand-Weeding

Even if you use landscape fabric or straw mulch, you'll need to weed by hand at some point. Here are some tips to make hand-weeding more enjoyable. And yes, I did just say that weeding can be enjoyable… I find it meditative, and there's a very high instant gratification factor.

+ Weed after a rain so that the soil is looser and softer.

+ Use a tool such as a butter knife in small spaces, and a hori hori knife in larger ones.

+ Get the root of the weed out too. No matter how many times you scrape off the sprout of a weed plant, it will continue to regrow because they're just that stubborn.

+ Carry a bucket along with you to collect the weeds, then discard them far away from the garden.

+ Wear knee pads. They look dorky, but your body will thank you.

+ Listen to an audiobook, music, or podcast while you weed, so your mind stays engaged while your hands are doing work. It makes the time go much faster.

Irrigation

Natural rainfall is the best source of water for plants because it contains wonderful nutrients like nitrogen and oxygen, and it also falls uniformly from the sky. Tap water does contain oxygen (albeit far less than rainwater), but it also contains added chemicals like chlorine and fluoride. Unfortunately, rainfall is not always regular enough to serve as the sole water source, especially during the summer months. Having a watering system set up when you plant is really important. I cannot tell you how many times I've told myself that I'll just set up the irrigation later, only to panic a few days after planting when my seedlings are drying out. I swear that one day I will learn this lesson!

The ideal system for watering is via drip irrigation or soaker hoses. Drip irrigation has so many benefits: it provides water directly to the roots of plants, has less evaporation, ensures reduced runoff, and discourages weeds since it only provides water to precise areas. Drip irrigation is highly efficient for both the environment and your physical labor, since you only have to set it up once a season. We lay drip irrigation lines directly on top of or underneath landscape fabric.

Overhead watering via sprinklers also works, as does a good ol' fashioned watering from a hose or watering can, especially if you have a water spigot nearby. It can be frustrating to get overhead sprinklers set up in the precise location to water your garden evenly. Watering cans require more physical labor because you walk back and forth to refill them, but they can be an efficient and precise system for a small garden. Another downside to overhead watering is that many plants do not benefit from having water sprayed directly onto their leaves or flowers, as it contributes to disease growth and can put water spots on flower petals.

Fertilizing

Although the dream is to have perfectly balanced soil with all the right nutrients, minerals, and microorganisms, that is unlikely to become a reality for most of us. Therefore, using some organic fertilizer helps feed your garden plants and keep them productive. We use several different types of organic fertilizer at Flourish. Before adding any type of fertilizer, it is important to refer to your soil test results and add the recommended N-P-K ratio (if you remember from soil testing back in Chapter 3, N-P-K refers to nitrogen, phosphorus, and potassium). Otherwise, you can unintentionally cause more harm than benefit.

1. **Granular organic all-purpose fertilizer:** Granular fertilizer is very easy to apply by hand, easy to come by at most gardening stores, and easy for plants to absorb. It needs to be applied about every month because it can be leached out of the soil. We spread granular fertilizer after planting so that it can be applied exactly at the base of the plants, thus reducing waste. A soil test will tell you how much fertilizer to apply per square foot, similar to how we calculated lime in Chapter 3.

2. **Liquid fertilizer:** Liquid fertilizer, such as fish emulsion or kelp, is easy to apply using either a backpack sprayer or a watering can. Liquid fertilizer should only be applied every other week, when there is no chance of rain for a least one day after application; otherwise, all your expensive fertilizer will just get washed away. Because the salts in fertilizers can sometimes damage leaves, liquid fertilizer should only be applied onto the bases of plants.

3. **Compost tea:** We make our own compost tea at Flourish using worm castings, kelp, alfalfa, and other trace nutrients. We combine all the ingredients in a fine mesh bag and let it bubble inside our compost tea brewer for about eighteen hours. Because compost tea is alive with microorganisms, it must be brewed using a bubbler to keep the tiny good guys supplied with oxygen, and it needs to be applied immediately. Using compost tea is more complicated and time-consuming than using other types of fertilizer, but it has the great benefit of microorganisms. We typically combine our homemade compost tea with liquid fertilizer in a backpack sprayer and apply them both at one time. Compost tea is sprayed directly onto the leaves of plants.

Plant Support

Once your plants are tall and full of blooms, they can easily topple over due to rain or wind. When that happens, it's almost impossible to get them upright again without breaking the stems. Having a good support system ensures that the stems will grow straight and tall. We begin supporting our plants when they're about two feet tall.

Netting

Because we grow a high volume of flowers at Flourish, netting is the most efficient way for us to support our plants. We use Tenax Hortonova netting with six-inch square holes; the plants easily grow up and through the netting, which provides support as the plants grow taller. We place two five-foot conduit posts on either side of the garden bed at six-foot intervals down the length of the entire bed. The netting is then suspended horizontally from the posts. The netting can be rolled up at the end of the season and reused for many years to come. We use netting on almost all of our flowers, but especially on snapdragons, zinnias, cosmos, scabiosas, and strawflowers.

Corralling

At Flourish, we use a system of corralling for our dahlia plants called the Florida Weave. The idea behind corralling is to sandwich the plants between lines of twine. Additional layers of twine can be added as the plants grow taller throughout the season. For smaller gardens, standalone supports such as tomato cages work great for staking individual plants.

Pinching

Pinching is when you snip out a portion of the new plant's growth, encouraging it to branch out instead of putting its energy into one central stem. Pinching is a concept that takes some getting used to—it feels almost criminal after spending so much time and energy getting your plants established, but I promise it's worth it! Pinching is best done when the plant has three to four sets of leaves. Keep in mind, though, that it's important to not remove more than 50 percent of its leaves, as that will inhibit the plant's ability to photosynthesize. Always cut the stem back to the next set of leaves, rather than leaving a bare stem sticking up in the center.

Not only does pinching encourage the plant to branch out, giving you more stems of flowers, it also encourages longer stems. For example, "cherry caramel" garden phlox will try to bloom when the plant is only one inch tall, so we snip off the buds three to four times in the late spring until the stems are long enough to use in an arrangement. By pinching our zinnias, we have over ten stems per single plant. That's a lot of flowers from one little seed!

However, not all flowers should be pinched. Pinching some plants, such as statice, some sunflowers, Canterbury bells, and lisianthuses, will cause the leaves to rosette and not grow tall. One-stem bloomers should not be pinched either—they only grow one stem! Other flowers like Queen Anne's lace, foxgloves, scabiosas, campanulas, delphiniums, ranunculi, and forget-me-nots naturally will grow multiple stems per plant and do not require pinching. It's great to experiment while you're still learning about your garden and see how plants behave differently when they are pinched versus not.

Here are some flowers that *do* benefit from pinching: anemones (pinch off the first, short blooms to encourage longer stems), zinnias, cosmos, dahlias, marigolds, phlox, snapdragons, celosias (the plume varieties), amaranth, globe amaranth, ageratum, and branching sunflowers.

Common Diseases Affecting Flowers

It would be impossible to address all the diseases that can destroy our lovingly grown flower gardens, but there are great resources available at your local Cooperative Extension Service Office for just about anything that pops up. We're going to focus on the two most common diseases that affect many flower growers: powdery mildew and botrytis.

Powdery Mildew

Powdery mildew is a fungal disease that affects tomatoes, melons, cucumbers, basil, roses, zinnias, dahlias, and many other tender annuals. Powdery mildew thrives in hot, humid climates and can spread from plant to plant via spores. Plant leaves will look like they've been dusted with flour, starting with white spots that eventually grow to cover entire leaves in a grayish white. Plants can survive while infected with powdery mildew, but they are much less productive. In extreme cases, it will kill the plants.

At Flourish, where we have hot and humid conditions all summer and most of the fall, some crops like zinnias become infected with powdery mildew every single year. This is one of the reasons why we succession plant zinnias—just as one planting becomes

infected and stops producing abundantly, another succession is ready to bloom. We just rip out the infected crop and add it to the burn pile (don't add affected plants to a compost pile because the disease can persist and spread). Providing good airflow by not overcrowding your plants and watering via drip irrigation are the best ways to prevent powdery mildew. If you do notice powdery mildew growing on your plants, it can be controlled by spraying an organically approved fungicide. We use MilStop (essentially a professional-grade baking soda solution) on crops like dahlias that cannot be succession planted. You can also create your own home remedy to control powdery mildew: mix one tablespoon of baking soda, one-half teaspoon of liquid soap, and one gallon of water. Spray liberally for several consecutive days on the infected leaves and repeat as needed.

Botrytis

Botrytis cinerea, also called grey mold, is a fungus that affects a huge variety of plants. There are so many strains of botrytis that it's hard to keep up, so you don't need to know the specifics. What you *do* need to know is that it can kill any part of your plant—stems, roots, buds, leaves, etc.—and it spreads very easily. It shows up as grey mushy spots on your plants and thrives in cool, damp environments. There really isn't a great way to control botrytis because it spreads so quickly, so it's best to remove the infected plants immediately and burn them. Some folks have reported success with biological fungicides, such as Serenade and Copper Soaps. Sadly, we lost an entire crop of perennial hybrid anemones during one intensely rainy year due to botrytis. Because the disease can live in the soil for years, we will not plant in that bed again for many years.

Beneficial Insects

Most bugs in the garden are actually good guys! Insects are beneficial for several reasons, including pollination and serving as predators by eating bad bugs. Here are the top five beneficial insects that we love having at Flourish:

+ **Ladybugs:** Besides being cute, ladybugs eat aphids (more on them in the next section). You can attract more ladybugs to your garden by planting dill or dandelion, but you can also buy live, dormant ladybugs from many home gardening stores or ARBICO Organics™ online and release them into your garden. Be sure to follow the directions on the container—if you release them at the wrong time of day, they will simply fly away, which isn't particularly helpful.

+ **Praying Mantises:** These are great predators and hunters that eat both good and bad guys in the garden. They love moths, grasshoppers, mosquitoes, roaches, flies, and aphids. Female praying mantises lay their eggs in an easily recognizable egg casing in the fall. When we discover an egg casing during the fall garden cleanup, we make sure to move it to a safe location off the ground.

+ **Earthworms:** Having earthworms in your soil is a sign that things are going well! They process organic matter by turning compost into nutrients and they improve the soil structure by adding tiny tunnels for roots to grow and air to flow. If you don't find many earthworms in your soil, you can dig them up from another part of your yard or buy them at home gardening stores or online.

+ **Green Lacewings:** The larvae of green lacewings eat thrips, aphids, leafhoppers, white flies, spider mites, and more. Green lacewings can be ordered from a reputable company specializing in integrated pest management, such as ARBICO Organics™.

+ **Soldier Beetles:** Soldier beetle larvae eat the eggs and larvae of beetles, grasshoppers, and moths. Adult soldier beetles also eat aphids. Fun fact: they are closely related to fireflies!

Common Garden Pests

Just like diseases, there are way too many pests to name that can threaten our gardens. Here are a handful of common culprits and some solutions:

+ **Aphids:** Aphids are tiny green insects that hang out on the stems of plants, literally sucking the life out of them. Aphids are super common, yet fairly easy to control. They can be sprayed off with water, but the best way to control them (in my opinion) is by introducing ladybugs. A few years ago, we had a serious aphid infestation on our foxglove patch. I released ladybugs one evening and, within two days, I could hardly find any aphids. Success!

+ **Japanese Beetles:** Japanese beetles are the bane of my existence in July. The beetles are actually neat looking, with a coppery green, iridescent head, but they do serious damage in the garden. They especially love garden roses, zinnias, and dahlias. Japanese beetles are grubs that spend months growing and living underground, emerging for about two months every

summer. They are very slow to move in the early morning, so we walk around the fields and pick off as many as possible and then drown them in soapy water. We also use pheromone traps to lure the beetles away from our flowers.

+ **Slugs:** Even though slugs are pretty cute with their miniature antennae, they love to munch on tender leaves and can wreak havoc seemingly overnight on hostas and dahlias. Slugs can be difficult to spot in the garden, but they leave behind a shiny trail of slime that is a telltale sign of their presence. The best ways to control slugs are by sprinkling a product called Sluggo around the base of your plants, and by keeping pathways free of garden debris.

+ **Grasshoppers:** Grasshoppers thrive in hot, dry conditions and love to munch on dahlias especially. The best way to combat grasshoppers is by creating a good habitat for their primary predators: birds and praying mantises.

+ **Deer:** Deer are so fickle! Honestly, I never trust that a plant is "deer resistant" because I believe that if deer want to eat something in your garden, they'll do as they please. The best method I've found to protect a garden from deer is fencing. We use a 3D-baited electric fence system on our farm. Basically, the bait on the electric fencing lures the deer in to lick the fence and they get shocked. This creates more of a psychological barrier rather than a physical barrier—deer are creatures of habit with established migration patterns, and this system teaches them to find somewhere else to migrate.

Chapter 6

Harvesting and Arranging Flowers

> **Tools:** *snips, bucket, vase, flower food, floral tape, rubber bands*

Now we finally get to my favorite part of gardening: cutting the flowers to both enjoy in your own home and share with others. I once gave a little bouquet of spring anemones to a contractor who had done work on our home. A few weeks later, he called just to tell me how much it meant to him, and that every time he looked at the flowers, he smiled. To me, there is no greater gift to give someone than making them smile!

Cut flowers require constant harvesting in order to keep blooming. A plant's natural cycle (a very distilled and oversimplified version) is to germinate, grow leaves, flower, get pollinated, produce seeds, and drop the seeds to replant itself again the next season. Once a flower drops its petals and begins growing seeds, it will not grow more flowers because it's focused on reproducing. It is important to understand this cycle because as cut flower gardeners, we want to help plants remain in the "grow leaves and flower" stage for as long as possible. We do this by continually harvesting and deadheading.

Harvesting

Each flower variety has a proper stage during which it should be harvested for longest vase life, to maximize hydration and ensure that it doesn't wilt immediately. It takes some time to learn the specific stage of harvest for each variety, but experimenting in your own garden is a great way to learn.

In general, flowers should be cut first thing in the morning or later in the evening. A flower maintains its maximum level of hydration during the cooler parts of the day, and our goal is to minimize the trauma of cutting the flower from its plant. Flowers should be cut at an angle using sharp, clean floral snips, then placed into clean water immediately. It's best to let the flowers rest in a cool, dark place right after harvesting so they can rehydrate.

Using flower food is important; bacteria are the primary cause of short vase lives in flowers, so the antibacterial agents in flower food and holding solution help control the growth of new bacteria. Think of the stem as a straw—a clean straw allows the cut flower to suck up as much water as it needs, helping it stay happy. The sugar in the flower food feeds the flower, since it's been removed from its nutrient source. When bacteria start growing in a vase or bucket, it causes the straw to gunk up, and the flower cannot drink as much or as easily. Clean buckets and vases are crucial! A good rule of thumb is that the bucket or vase should be clean enough that you would drink out of it yourself. Removing the leaves that are immersed in water at the bottom of the stem helps reduce the growth of bacteria.

It can be difficult to know where to cut on the stem of a flower and, similar to pinching, it can feel hard to cut a lot off the plants. But cutting deeply with the bloom on long stems will only encourage the plants to grow longer stems in the future. I promise it's worth it! For the first cut, I recommend leaving a minimum stem length of twelve inches for most flowers; any shorter than this and the stems are not long enough to arrange. Although each flower variety has different growth habits, stems between eighteen and thirty-six inches are generally the standard for flower sales.

Harvesting for Cut Flower Sales

At Flourish, we carry buckets of water into the field with us while harvesting so the flowers can go straight into clean water. We add a little holding solution to the water in each bucket; the holding solution is similar to flower food in that it contains an antibacterial agent and sugar, but it contains less sugar than flower food. Because we are harvesting the flowers to sell, we want to halt the process of blooming so that our customers have the longest flower blooming experience. Flower stems are rubber banded into bunches of ten stems each. The buckets of flowers are immediately placed into our floral cooler to rest for several hours before we arrange with them. I believe that a floral cooler is a must-have for flower growers who want to produce a high-quality product.

Deadheading

Sometimes the flowers seem to all bloom at once and it's impossible to cut them at the proper stage of harvest. This is where deadheading comes into play. Deadheading is different from harvesting in that you do not need to cut a long stem. The purpose is to remove just one bloom from the plant to keep it in the blooming stage of its life cycle and keep it from producing seeds. Cut down to the next lower set of leaves, just below the bloom.

Admittedly, deadheading is very difficult for some people to understand—my husband and mother being two of those people. Even after many years of growing flowers professionally, my husband still asks me why I can't sell those

flowers instead of deadheading them. My mother practically cries over the deadheaded flowers and tries to save them all from the compost pile (even though I keep her in good supply of healthy flowers).

At Flourish, we refer to deadheading as "blossom promotion." By cutting off any flowers that are past their prime, we are helping the plants quickly grow new blooms and are able to harvest from them for months.

Arranging

You could ask ten different floral designers about their flower arrangement approach and you would receive ten different answers. There is no right or wrong way to arrange flowers! Flowers are inherently beautiful, and so is the end result of an arrangement. Some methods and principles will help you create beautiful, balanced arrangements; the more you practice designing with intention, the more pleased you will be with the arrangements. Sustainability is a priority for my designs, just as it is in operating the farm. Even when designing for large weddings with huge, hanging floral installations, we use materials that are reusable or decompose easily.

Paying attention to small details while designing will beautifully impact your arrangements. The nuances of foliage color, leaf shape and size, stem color, varying shades in the center of a bloom or on the edges of its petals—train your eye to notice all of these little accents.

Centerpiece with Chicken Wire

Tools: *floral snips, waterproof floral tape, vase, chicken wire, wire cutters, flower food*

Choosing a Vase: There are so many options to choose from, but the most important thing to keep in mind is that whatever vessel you choose must be watertight and clean. When I create a simple arrangement to give as a gift or for my own dining room table, I prefer vases with wide mouths that are about six to eight inches tall. Don't be afraid to think outside the box when it comes to flower vases. Vintage pitchers, local pottery, and even old flowerpots make for unique vases.

Ingredients: It's important to incorporate a mixture of different elements to create a balanced and interesting arrangement. Here is my recipe for a well-balanced arrangement:

+ Three to five focal flowers: peonies or garden roses in the spring; sunflowers or dahlias in the summer and fall (some of my favorites).

+ Three to four tall flowers or spikes: snapdragons or foxgloves in the spring; celosias or delphiniums in the summer and fall.

+ Five to seven round, disc flowers: ranunculi or anemones in the spring; marigolds, sweet Williams, or zinnias in the summer and fall.

+ Four to five filler flowers: forget-me-nots or phlox in the spring; Queen Anne's lace or globe amaranth in the summer and fall.

+ Four to five whimsical, airy elements: scabiosa, cosmos, dill, and wild grasses.

+ Seven to ten sprigs of greenery: herbs, hostas, forsythia, viburnum, dusty miller, and lamb's ear are perfect home-garden staples to include in your arrangement. "Weeds" such as honeysuckle and privet are some of my favorite, long-lasting greenery.

+ Don't be afraid to add unexpected elements into your bouquet, such as artichokes, vines, and unripe berries. Floral arrangements are not limited to just flowers!

Designing:

1. It's a good idea to have a color palette in mind for your arrangement before you purchase your flowers, or you can wait and let one specific flower provide the inspiration. For example, a coral charm peony may be the perfect inspiration for a spring arrangement. I'd choose colors that would accentuate my peony, such as pale pink ranunculi, white and peach poppies with a yellow center, white sweet peas, pale pink snapdragons, bright green hostas, and honeysuckle vines. I prefer not to use flowers that are all exactly the same hue.

2. Prepare the vase. Loosely fold a square of chicken wire about two times the size of the mouth of the vase and place it down into the vase. It's important not to squeeze the chicken wire into a ball—there needs to be plenty of space for the stems to poke through. Create a grid with floral tape on the top of the vase. This will help your arrangement maintain a solid structure. Fill the vase about three-quarters full of water and add a sprinkle of flower food.

3. Begin with the greenery, placing it around the outer edge of the vase in a triangle, and one to two sprigs in the middle of the grid.

4. Use the spike flowers to create a swooping shape.

5. Place the focal flowers equidistant around the vase, accentuating the triangle shape of the greenery. I prefer using asymmetrical numbers of flowers and layering them to create a stair-step effect.

6. Turn the vase as you work so each of its sides receives attention. A lazy Susan comes in handy here!

7. Add clusters of round and filler flowers to fill in the gaps between the focal flowers. Add them in, one stem at a time, so you can see where the gaps are in the arrangement. Sometimes it's best to use neutral filler flowers around your focal flower to really let it pop. I also love stair-stepping the round flowers to create depth and dimension.

8. Finally, add the wispy, airy elements. Place these on opposite sides of the vase or dangling over the edge. Beware of creating a bunny ear effect, though!

9. Once I've completed an arrangement, I always walk away for a few minutes so I can come back with fresh eyes. I will almost always notice a gap that I didn't see before or find something that I want to adjust. It is also helpful to snap a photo of the arrangement to look at it from a different perspective.

Centerpiece with a Pin Frog

> **Tools:** *floral snips, vase, pin frog, floral putty, flower food*

Choosing a Vase: When designing with a pin frog, I love using shallow, wide vessels to create loose, whimsical arrangements. Any watertight vessel that you can reach your hand into the bottom will also work fine.

Ingredients: It's important to incorporate a mixture of different elements to create a balanced and interesting arrangement. Here is my recipe for a well-balanced arrangement:

+ Eight to ten focal flowers: peonies or garden roses in the spring; dahlias in the summer and fall.

+ Five to six tall flowers or spikes: snapdragons, celosias, delphiniums, tuberoses, amaranth, or nicotianas.

+ Five to seven round, disc flowers: ranunculi, anemones, marigolds, strawflowers, or zinnias.

+ Four to five filler flowers: forget-me-nots, phlox, chocolate lace flowers, ageratum, or ammi.

+ Four to five whimsical, airy elements: scabiosas, cosmos, silenes, toad lilies, columbines, nigellas, hybrid anemones, and wild grasses.

+ Seven to ten stems of greenery and vines: herbs, hostas, baptisia, forsythia, viburnum, ninebark, mountain mint, and elaeagnus.

Designing

1. Cover the back of the pin frog with floral putty. Place the frog at the bottom of a dry vase. Using a rag to protect your hand, push down on the frog and turn it to both secure it to the bottom of vase and release any trapped air bubbles. Fill the vase about three-quarters full with water and add flower food.

2. Begin by adding the largest, heaviest branches of greenery first to create a whimsical shape in a tripod pattern. Push these stems firmly into the center of the pin frog. Echo the shape of the greenery with spike flowers, securing them toward the center of the pin frog.

3. Place the focal flowers equidistant around the vase, accentuating the tripod shape of the greenery. I prefer using asymmetrical numbers of flowers and layering them to create a stair-step effect. Be sure that each stem is secured in the pin frog by pushing with a gentle firmness. You may not be able to place stems directly into the frog once it is full, but the web of stems within the vase should start to provide good stability as more stems are added.

4. Add clusters of round and filler flowers to fill in the gaps between the focal flowers. Stair-step the round flowers to create depth and dimension.

5. Add the whimsical elements. Place these on opposite sides of your vase or dangling over the edge.

6. Finally, add draping vines or unripe berries to hang over the edge of the vase.

Hand-Tied Bouquet

Tools: *floral snips, tape, tall vase with a wide mouth*

Designing bouquets is my absolute favorite thing to do with flowers! There is just something magical about taking all the loose ingredients and turning them into a bouquet for a bride, bridesmaid, or just for fun. Designing bouquets begins with choosing a color palette and your ingredients.

Ingredients:

+ Five to six stems of focal flowers: I begin by choosing my focal flower first, that way I can select other ingredients with complimentary shapes, sizes, and textures to enhance the focal flowers. Favorite focal blooms include peonies, garden roses, Italian poppies, bearded irises, and dahlias.

+ Seven to eight stems of secondary focal flowers: These flowers add tons of interest, depth, and romance to the bouquet, but are smaller in size than the focal flowers. I love using flowers with ruffled or pronounced petals as a secondary focal. Favorites include ranunculi, anemones, zinnias, hellebores, rudbeckias, lisianthuses, and strawflowers.

+ Five to seven stems of spikes: Flowers with an elongated shape add structure and lines to the bouquet. Favorites include snapdragons, campanulas, celosias, larkspur, delphiniums, foxgloves, Veronicas, and astilbes.

+ Eight to nine stems of dainty filler: Filler provides a platform to support the "showier" blooms, but also adds depth, interest, and weight. Favorites include dianthus, orlaya, Queen Anne's lace, forget-me-not, saponaria, globe amaranth, ageratum, hydrangea, rudbeckia triloba, yarrow, and phlox.

+ Ten to twelve stems of greenery: Greenery can serve the purposes of many of the other elements because it provides the bouquet with structure, texture, and filler. It also provides a lovely contrast to the flowers. Favorites include mint, shiso, eucalyptus, viburnum, ninebark,

elaeagnus, nandina, ferns, forsythia, scented geranium, raspberry foliage, and Solomon's seal.

✦ Six to seven stems of whimsy: The whimsy is my favorite aspect of the bouquet because it is what makes the bouquet dance in your hands. Favorites include cosmos, chocolate cosmos, columbine, nicotiana, hybrid anemone, Astrantia, geum, clematis, and scabiosa.

✦ Three to five textural elements: The sky's the limit when it comes to adding texture into a bouquet! Some of the best textural elements come from foraging in my yard or along the side of the road. Favorites include unripe blueberries, snowberries, grasses, poppy pods, amaranthuses, succulents, lilacs, dill, and scabiosa pods.

Designing:

1. Begin by laying out all your ingredients on the worktable, then separate them into piles by flower type and by color.

2. Process the flowers and greenery by stripping off three-quarters of the leaves, leaving just the top of the flower. The leaves and branches will become hidden in the bouquet and only get in the way. I take care to snip off anything useable, like side buds and small branches of greenery, for other arrangements later (like short-bud vases and boutonnieres).

3. Begin by making a cluster of filler flowers and greenery. Take care not to use your favorite stems because this cluster will be hidden inside the interior of the bouquet.

4. Add one ingredient at a time, laying each new stem at an angle across the other stems already in the bouquet. After adding a stem, turn the bouquet slightly to add the next stem in a new place.

Take care to not add stems lower or higher than what is already in your hand. This will create an uneven effect in the bouquet, or make it look as if one side is sloping downward.

5. Keep in mind the rule of thirds when placing each category of ingredient. For example, do not cluster all of your focal blooms on one side; instead, space them into different quadrants of the bouquet. Use the same principle when adding secondary focal blooms.

6. Use the filler and greenery to create distance and depth between the bigger blooms.

7. Thread in the whimsy at the very end so it has the maximum ability to dance and wiggle in the bouquet (but not so much so that it looks goofy).

8. Use a mirror to inspect your bouquet as you design so that you can more easily notice any holes or places that are overcrowded.

9. It's always nice to have another person hold the bouquet once you think it may be done so that you can get an even better perspective.

10. Once you are done, cut the stems so they are even.

Paper-Wrapped Market Bouquet

> **Tools:** *floral snips, scissors, rubber bands, brown kraft paper*

Designing a market bouquet is similar to designing a hand-tied bouquet, but it is simpler overall and comes together more quickly. Wrapped market bouquets are designed to be aesthetically pleasing, neatly packaged for the recipient to take home and place in their favorite vase. The recipe below contains quantities that we typically use at Flourish for our grocery store and flower bouquet subscriptions; these quantities can easily be doubled or tripled to make an oversized bouquet for a special occasion. When selecting flowers for a market bouquet, I primarily use blooms that are not fully open (or are in the cracking bud stage for flowers like cosmos, sunflowers, and poppies) so that the customer or recipient receives a bouquet with the longest vase life possible. However, I also include at least one fully open bloom of each variety so that the bouquet still looks visually appealing and draws the customer in. While I may use some extra special and beautiful blooms with short vase lives in a hand-tied bouquet, I only use blooms that have long vase lives for market bouquets.

Ingredients:

+ One to three stems of focal flowers: peonies, garden roses, Italian poppies, sunflowers, or dahlias.

+ Five to six stems of secondary focal flowers: ranunculi, anemones, zinnias, rudbeckias, lisianthuses, strawflowers, or marigolds.

+ Three to four stems of spikes: snapdragons, campanulas, celosias, larkspur, delphiniums, foxgloves, or amaranth.

+ Five to six stems of filler: dianthus, orlaya, Queen Anne's lace, forget-me-not, saponaria, globe amaranth, ageratum, rudbeckia triloba, yarrow, chocolate lace flower, and phlox.

+ Three to four stems of greenery: mint, shiso, eucalyptus, viburnum, ninebark, elaeagnus, nandina, fern, forsythia, scented geranium, raspberry foliage, and Solomon's seal.

+ Four to five stems of whimsy: cosmos, chocolate cosmos, nicotiana, hybrid anemone, geum, sweet pea on the vine, scabiosa, dill, and other textural elements.

Designing:

1. Begin by laying out all your ingredients on the worktable, then separate them into piles by flower type.

2. Strip off half the leaves, leaving the bottom half of the stems exposed.

3. Begin by picking up one or two stems of a focal flower and two stems of greenery. Hold them in your nondominant hand and use the greenery to separate the stems of focal flowers.

4. Add the filler evenly around the bouquet. After adding one stem, turn the bouquet slightly to add the next stem in a different place.

5. Next, add in the spikes evenly around the bouquet. It is important to place almost all of the stems on the same plane, so the bouquet has a nice dome or flat shape at the top.

6. Add the secondary focal flowers, clustering two stems together with one stem slightly higher (about one inch) than the other. This creates a little more depth within the bouquet, while maintaining the dome shape at the top. Place the secondary focal flowers evenly around the bouquet.

7. Add in another focal flower if you are using multiple stems. Add any remaining stems of greenery evenly around the bouquet.

8. Add the whimsy last and place it slightly (about one to two inches) above the main dome of the bouquet.

9. Once you are done, cut the stems so they are even. Secure the bouquet with a rubber band. At Flourish, we include a small packet of flower food with every market bouquet and secure it to the stems with a rubber band.

10. Cut a rectangle of kraft paper and fold it at an angle. Place the top of the bouquet in the "v" of the folded paper. Fold one side over the other to frame the dome of the bouquet—it should be wrapped securely enough so the paper doesn't slip down, but not so tight as to compress the blooms. Secure the loose ends with a sticker, some tape, or a staple.

Chapter 7

Putting the Garden to Bed

Tools: *shovel, pitchfork, gloves, clippers, loppers, crate*

The first frost in the fall signals the end of another season in the flower garden. A frost will cause all tender annuals to die—even if the plants look fine in the morning, their leaves will be blackened by noon. The frost is always bittersweet for me: I am sad to see the flowers go, but also grateful for the start of a slower-paced season. The days of early-rise harvesting and never-ending weeding are over. Yet, there is still so much to do in order to ensure a successful season the next year!

Garden Bed Cleanup

After the annual flowers are killed by the frost, it's time to start removing them from the garden.

+ We begin by taking down all the support netting and rolling it up to use again next year. Remove all the posts from the garden area too.

+ Next, pull all the plants up (we do this by hand) and shake the soil loose from the roots. Some plants seem to pop right out of the ground, and some are stubborn as can be. Think of it as a great workout! Add the dead plants to the compost or burn piles.

+ Carefully roll up the drip irrigation lines so they can be reused next year.

+ Use a backpack blower to remove loose soil and leaves from the landscape fabric.

+ Roll up the landscape fabric, leaving the staples secured to the fabric. This saves a step next year.

+ We lightly work the soil with a disc harrow to break up any compaction (a shallow pass with the rototiller works, too).

+ Spread cover crop seed (more on cover crops later in this chapter).

Composting

Creating a compost pile near your garden creates a space to dispose of dead garden plants that will provide you with organic material for years. Remember to never add diseased plants to your compost pile—diseased plant material should be burned instead. Choose a spot for your compost pile away from your home, where it won't be an eyesore and where you won't be bothered by the smell. Decomposing plants are stinky.

Composting requires three basic ingredients: brown stuff like dead leaves, plants, and branches; green stuff like fruit and vegetable scraps, grass clippings, and coffee grounds; and water to help these materials decompose. Materials that you can add to your compost include fruits and vegetables, eggshells, coffee grounds and filters, tea bags, nut shells, newspaper, cardboard, printer paper, leaves, sawdust, wood chips, dryer lint, hair and pet fur, and fireplace ashes. It is important to *not* add meat, dairy products, or other animal products to the compost.

Begin a compost pile by layering the greens and browns. If you live in an especially dry climate, water the pile about once a week. The smaller the size of the stuff you add to the pile, the more easily it will decompose. Earthworms are an integral part of the composting process. If your compost pile is on the ground, earthworms will crawl in and join the party. If you are composting in a closed container, such as a barrel, add in earthworms by either digging them from the yard or buying them.

The natural process of decomposition takes time—anywhere from two months to several years. The stuff at the bottom of the pile will be ready first, so it's a good idea to check the pile every few months. Remove the finished compost when it's very dark in color and crumbly.

Cover Crops

A cover crop is a plant that is grown to cover the soil, rather than to be harvested. It is grown *for* the soil. Cover crops are typically legumes (peas and clover) and grasses (rye, oats, and wheat). I love growing cover crops, and they are a very important aspect of our farming operation—one that keeps our soil healthy and our growing practices sustainable. I'm going to be completely honest though…I do not know the in-depth science behind it, and (please don't judge me here) I actually don't care to geek out on it. I just know that cover cropping is wonderful and helps keep my soil healthy.

Why You Should Use Cover Crops

Even science-deficient farmers like me should know the *why*, so here are the oversimplified basics of why it's important to cover crop:

1. There are millions and billions of tiny organisms and good bacteria living in the soil. It's our job as farmers to keep those guys happy so that they in turn keep our flower crops healthy and happy. Those good little guys need to eat, and cover crop material provides them with the nutrients and minerals they need to stay happy and alive. Happy organisms = happy crops.

2. Increasing organic matter in the soil is a never-ending project. All plants take nutrients out of the soil throughout their growth cycles, and those nutrients need to be replenished for the next season. It's like eating a hearty meal the night before running a marathon. This is basically the same theory as reason number one, but with a different spin. Some flower varieties "feed" more heavily on minerals and nutrients, and cover crops (planted after those flowers are done growing for the season) add those much-needed minerals and nutrients back into the soil, making it more fertile. For example, peas/legumes are great for adding in nitrogen. Our soil tends to be heavy with clay here in western North Carolina, so organic matter helps lighten things up.

3. Erosion control! We farm on a large slope at Flourish and losing precious topsoil is always a concern. Loose dirt is more likely to wash away during heavy rain, so having plants with roots growing (a.k.a., cover crops or actual crops) helps keep the soil in place. One of my goals is to never have a field or bed empty on the farm for more than a month. Side note, erosion is another reason why we use landscape fabric in our pathways! It's a win-win because it keeps soil in place during rain storms and helps with weed control.

4. Weed control! Rather than leaving a field bare for part of the season, thus giving weeds free rein to grow abundantly, cover crops sown at the right time can outcompete the weeds. I would much rather have a field full of buckwheat than weeds!

5. The crops can serve as a habitat for beneficial insects and bees!

Cover crops are grown strictly for these benefits. They are not grown to harvest the seeds or for eating. In fact, it is very important that cover crops are cut down before they even reach the stage where they produce seeds. If you let a cover crop go to seed, then you have unintentionally seeded your entire garden bed with a plant that will compete with your flowers the next year.

Preparing a Garden Plot for a Cover Crop

The two mains seasons during which I plant cover crops are late spring/early summer after our cold-hardy annuals finish blooming, and late fall after the first frost.

After following the steps previously outlined in "Garden Bed Cleanup," we do one pass with our disc harrow using the tractor. This loosens up the soil and makes a nice home for the seed without disturbing it too much. The same results can be accomplished on a small scale with a hard-tined rake. Once that's done, the field is ready for you to spread cover crop seed. I look at the weather forecast and aim to sow seed right before rain is expected. I spread the seed by hand while carrying a five-gallon bucket. There are certainly fancier, less labor-intensive methods of spreading cover crop seed, but this works for us. We farm on a slope which makes it too difficult to use a push-type broadcast spreader on the uphill. We also don't have a fancy broadcaster for behind the tractor (plus, we try to minimize the amount we drive the tractor in the fields to lessen compaction), so the old-fashioned way gets it done.

Spring and Fall Cover Crops

Here's a very simple breakdown of what and we plant and when:

Summer: Buckwheat, Cowpeas, Sudangrass

After hardy spring flowers (like snapdragons, feverfew, dianthus, ranunculi, etc.) are done blooming, we prepare the beds using the method described above. Cover crops (especially buckwheat) serve as great forage for the bees over the summer and grow quickly, giving us ample time to have those beds ready for fall planting. We typically mow/cut down summer cover crops in late summer and then let the plants die back for about one to two weeks (this timing all depends on the weather and how busy we are with other farm tasks). We use our disc harrow to incorporate the cover crop debris into the soil and then make the beds smooth with the tiller. We then lay drip lines and landscape fabric, and the beds are ready for planting. This area usually ends up being planted with cold-hardy annuals once again. While there are certainly many other summer cover crops that can be grown, buckwheat is quick and easy and has become my go-to. I always make sure to leave a few fall-prepared beds empty and ready to go, so that I'm not too stressed looking for available planting space in the early spring.

Late Fall/Early Winter: Austrian Winter Peas, Winter Rye, Hairy Vetch, Winter Oats, Clover

After the summer annuals have been killed by a hard frost, we prepare the beds using the same method. Winter peas, rye, and vetch are a great mix for easy winter cover cropping, though I switch up my mixture a little each year and use oats, winter wheat, clover, and radishes. These crops will grow slowly throughout the winter and will then start to take off during those warm spring days. We usually mow these cover crops in mid-spring so that we can prepare the bed for planting tender summer annuals.

A local feed and seed store is a great source for cover crop seed. It's usually sold by the pound, and employees will often help you decide which mix to use in your garden. Aim for sixty pounds of seed per acre, four to five pounds per thousand square feet, or four ounces per hundred square feet. Cover crops are great for small garden beds too! Rather than letting garden beds sit empty all winter, planting a cover crop is an all-natural, inexpensive way to add nutrients into the soil and provide a food source for insects.

Deep Dive: Digging Dahlia Tubers

Dahlia tubers can be successfully overwintered (or oversummered) in warm climates, but it's always a gamble to leave them in the ground for the entire year. Dahlia tubers are especially prone to rotting and freezing, so we always dig up our tubers at Flourish. Plus, dahlia tubers multiply underground–by digging them up each year, you can increase your stock for the following season. If you live in a warm climate where the ground never freezes and there's not much rain to cause the tubers to rot, you can successfully leave your tubers in the ground all year round. If you are in a warm climate and do not wish to dig up your tubers, then you can stop the "to do" list after cutting the dead growth off down to the ground.

+ After the first frost, allow the plants to remain as they are in the garden for several weeks (yes, they'll look dead). This period of time allows the tubers to gather sugar to help them sprout again the following year.

+ After a few weeks, cut all the dead growth off down to ground level.

+ Carefully lift the tubers out of the soil using a shovel or pitchfork. Take extra care not to stab them or accidentally cut them in half.

+ Remove as much soil from the tubers as possible and place them inside a milk crate or container with holes for airflow.

+ Store the crates in a basement, garage, or shed. Somewhere cool (but not freezing), dark, and with good airflow is extremely important; I often set a box fan on low to keep the air circulating around the crates of tubers. Choose a location where you can ensure the temperature doesn't drop below 45 degrees Fahrenheit/7 degrees Celsius. You don't want those tubers to freeze! Also, anywhere that is prone to mildew and moisture is not a good choice.

+ Check the tubers every month during storage for mold. If you notice a small amount of mold growing, the tubers can be lightly sprayed with diluted bleach. Remove any tubers that show signs of rot.

Other Fall Garden Chores

There are a few other chores that are important when tucking the garden in before winter arrives:

✦ Plants like baptisia, sedum, peonies, columbine, and clematis should be pruned in the fall to make way for new growth in the spring. We add a fresh layer of compost onto garden roses, hellebores, and peonies to help them stay cozy over the winter.

✦ If you live in a climate with consistently freezing temperatures, remove any water from hoses and irrigation lines so they do not burst. An air compressor works well for this.

✦ Clean and sharpen tools and secure any materials that can blow away. It's so satisfying to have everything tidy and in a safe place during winter, ready to use again in the spring.

✦ Do an inventory of supplies, such as irrigation lines and fittings, snips, buckets, flower food, etc. Order any needed supplies over the winter so they are readily available in the spring.

Keep Growing Flowers

Growing flowers will be a lifelong labor of love, with each season bringing different challenges, successes, and lessons. Part of what I love about gardening and flower farming is that it's never boring! By the time the garden cleanup is complete, I am longing for slower-paced winter days of sipping tea and reading books by the fire. My winter hibernation usually only lasts about a month before I begin missing the flowers terribly. Thank goodness each new season provides a clean slate to begin again, to try new things, and to experiment with growing new flowers.

Tools

1. Stirrup hoe
2. Pruners
3. Shovel
4. Measuring wheel
5. Pitchfork
6. Waterproof tape
7. Holly Chapple pillow cage
8. Chicken wire
9. Stem wrap
10. Bind wire
11. Floral putty
12. Paddle Wire
13. Water tubes
14. Rubber bands
15. Pin frogs
16. Watering can
17. Floral snips
18. Rose thorn remover
19. Baler twine
20. Sod staples
21. Garden marker
22. Garden pot stakes
23. Bulb planter
24. Copper stakes
25. Hand pruners
26. Butter knife
27. Hori hori
28. Trowel
29. Knee pads
30. Garden gloves
31. Widger
32. Hand seeder
33. Plug tray labels
34. 1020 tray
35. 128 cell plug tray
36. 72 cell plug tray

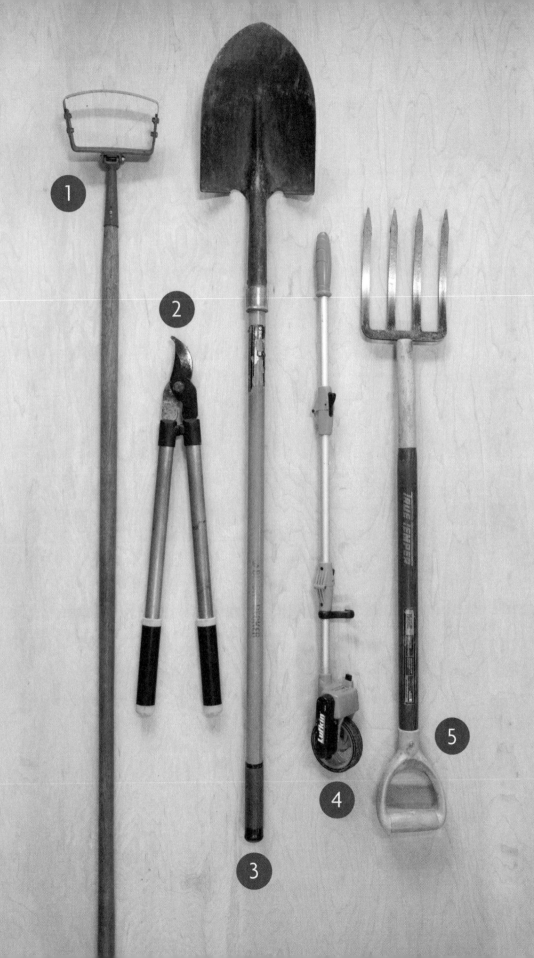

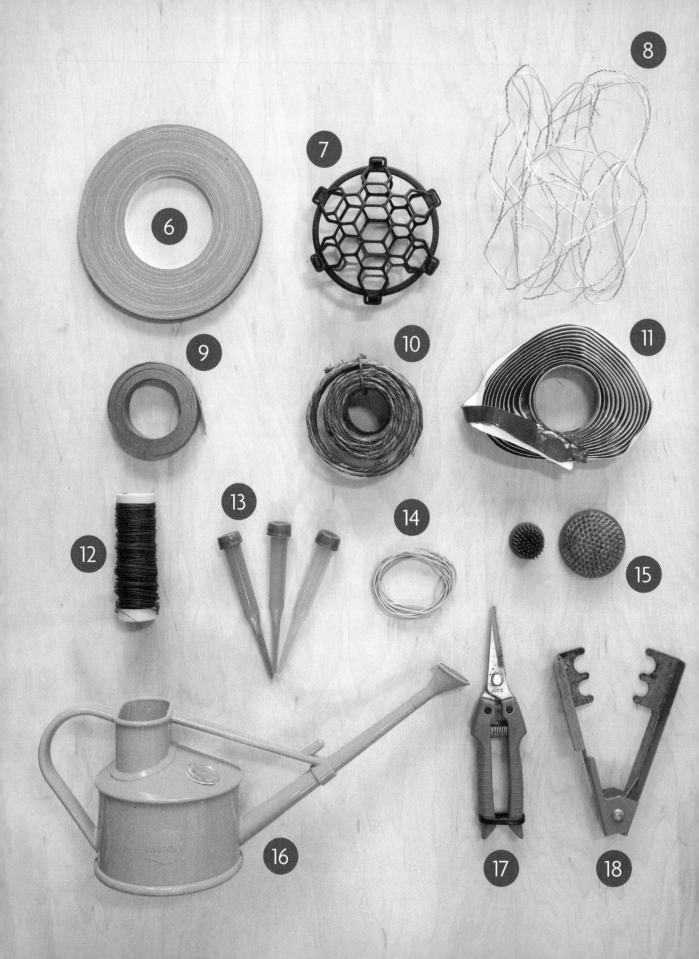

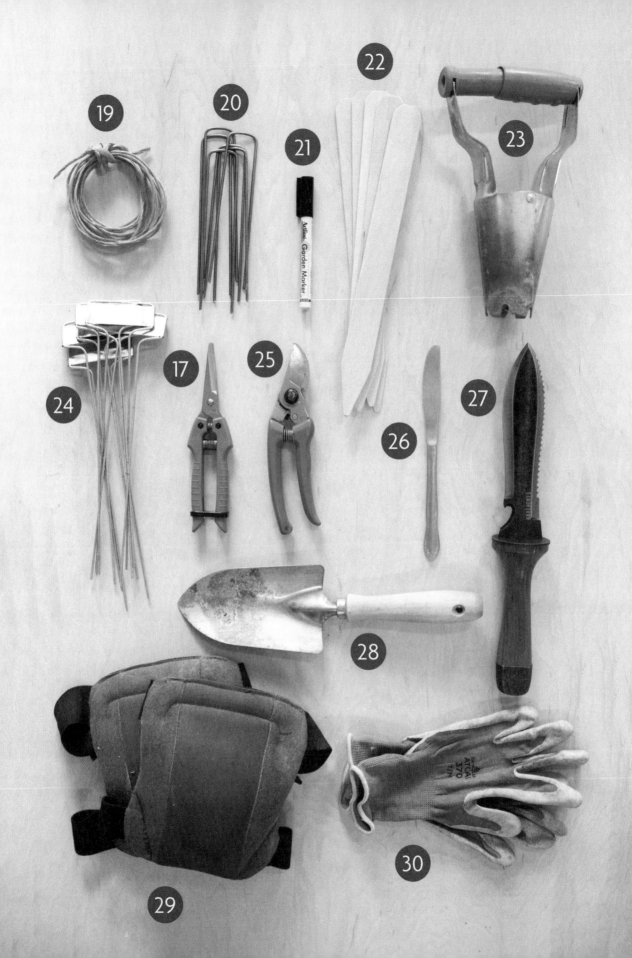

Resources

Seeds, Bulbs, & Tubers

Flourish Flower Farm
www.flourishflowerfarm.com
Ranunculus and anemone corms, dahlia tubers, and spring flowering bulbs.

Johnny's Selected Seeds
www.johnnyseeds.com
Seeds, tools, and resources catering to home gardeners and professional growers.

Renee's Garden
www.reneesgarden.com
Seeds for flowers, vegetables, and herbs for home gardeners.

Eden Brothers
www.edenbrothers.com
Online retailer catering to home gardeners for seeds, bulbs, ranunculus and anemone corms, and dahlia tubers.

Fred C. Gloeckner & Co.
www.fredgloeckner.com
Broker for seeds, plugs, bulbs, tubers, rooted cuttings, supplies, and more. Larger quantities available for professional growers.

Farmer Bailey
www.farmerbailey.com
Broker of annual and perennial plugs for professional growers.

Geo Seed
www.geoseed.com
Large quantities of seed for professional growers.

Swan Island Dahlias
www.dahlias.com
Huge variety of dahlia tubers for home gardeners.

Flower-Growing Tools & Supplies

A.M. Leonard Horticultural Tool & Supply Co.

www.amleo.com

Tools and supplies, especially for horticulture.

Farmer's Friend LLC

www.farmersfriend.com

Hoop houses/caterpillar tunnels, silage tarps, landscape fabric, frost covers, sandbags, and irrigation supplies.

FarmTek

www.farmtek.com

Supplies for seed starting, tags and labels, hoop houses, shade cloth, and more.

Rain-Flo Irrigation

www.rainfloirrigation.com

Drip irrigation systems and supplies, row covers/frost cloths, frost cloth hoops, and sandbags.

Griffin Greenhouse Supplies, Inc.

www.griffins.com

Landscape fabric, potting soil, organic fertilizer, and so much more.

Ground Cover Industries, Inc.

www.landscapefabric.com

Landscape fabric and frost protection. Use code 'flourishflowers' for 10 percent off!

Home Improvement Stores or Amazon

- ✦ Tenax Hortonova Netting

- ✦ A half-inch EMT conduit

- ✦ Chicken wire

- ✦ Chrysal and FloraLife flower food products

ARBICO Organics™

www.arbico-organics.com

Integrated Pest Management specialists and online sales of beneficial insects.

Floral Design Tools & Supplies

Jamali Garden

www.jamaligarden.com

Unique vases for retail and wholesale.

Floral Supply Syndicate

www.fss.com

Wholesale supplier of bulk vases, containers, candles, flower food, wire, tools, floral tape, and more.

Accent Decor, Inc.

www.accentdecor.com

Wholesale supplier of unique vases, candlesticks, and more.

Continuing Education

Association of Specialty Cut Flower Growers

www.ascfg.org

Trade organization for professional cut flower growers. An incredible educational resource!

Slow Flowers

www.slowflowers.com

A community of florists, suppliers, and flower growers dedicated to supporting domestic, US-grown flowers.

Acknowledgements

There are so many kind people who have supported me and Flourish Flower Farm, who have helped to literally grow the farm and business from a dream to a reality. I am especially grateful to those who helped this book reach your hands. Thank you to Lisa McGuinness, my editor at Mango Publishing and Yellow Pear Press, for giving me an opportunity to channel my creative energy and years of experience into this book. Lisa's guidance and encouragement were incredible gifts. Thank you to Debra Prinzing for enthusiastically agreeing to write the foreword, and more importantly, for being the voice, champion, and point of connection for domestic flower farms and floral designers through Slow Flowers. Debra, you are my hero!

Thank you to our small yet mighty Flourish Flower Farm team—Hali, Allison, Dylan, and our group of dedicated freelancers—for working so hard with positive attitudes and for your attention to detail. You are the true hearts and hands of Flourish! Thank you to Tonya Engelbrecht for beautifully photographing the farm over the course of an entire year, for making even the "less scenic" shots look lovely, and for being excited about my endless shot lists. Thank you to Meghan Rolfe Ogburn for beautifully photographing every stage and location of Flourish since our first year, and for your continued friendship and business partnership. Thank you also to Julia and Thomas Berolzheimer and Sarah Collier for contributing beautiful photos from your visits to the farm over the years.

Thank you to the Flourish family of workshop guests, florists and floral designers, grocery stores, private session clients, wedding clients, followers on social media, and everyone else who supports this small business by buying our flowers and cheering us on. Thank you to my circle of friends who are like family for being a sounding board, as well as a source of inspiration, love, and encouragement—and for still being my friend even though you rarely see me during flower-growing season! Thank you to the Thompsons at Our Fiddlehead Farm for being our chosen family and farming partners. I am grateful to be doing life alongside you.

Thank you to my immediate and extended family for your unconditional love and for creating a safe space for me to follow my dreams. A special thank you to my parents for teaching me the value of honest, hard work, and for instilling in me a love of and respect for nature. And finally, thank you to my husband William for his belief in me, his hard work every single day, his wisdom, silliness, and love. Life simply wouldn't be as enjoyable without you…you are my everything.

About the Author

Niki Irving is the flower farmer and florist of Flourish Flower Farm, a nine-acre specialty cut flower farm nestled in the Blue Ridge Mountains of Asheville, North Carolina. Niki grows over three hundred varieties of cut flowers and foliage and creates seasonally inspired designs for weddings and special events. Niki loves growing, nurturing, and creating beauty and believes that flowers make the world a more beautiful, joyful place. She is an active member of the Association of Specialty Cut Flower Growers and Slow Flowers and has been featured in numerous national publications. She sells her flowers wholesale locally and nationally, plus hosts floral design and flower farming workshops on her farm. Niki tends the flowers alongside her husband William.

Index

Anemone 27, 53, 57, 59, 62, 77-80, 95, 101, 107, 111, 115-116, 119-120, 141

Annuals 26-27, 29-30, 34, 47-48, 51-52, 54, 57, 61, 85, 93, 123, 128-130

  Hardy 26-27, 30, 48, 51, 57, 61, 128-129

  Tender 27, 29, 51, 57, 93, 123, 130

Beneficial Insects 95-96, 128, 143

Biennials 27, 29

Bouquet 15, 17, 19, 62, 101, 108, 117-121

  Hand-tied bouquet 115-117

  Paper-Wrapped Market Bouquet 119-121

  Planting for a Balanced Bouquet 62

Bulbs 26-27, 29-30, 47, 51, 63-64, 68, 73-74, 77, 141

Centerpiece 15, 107-108, 111-112

  Chicken wire 107-108

  Pin Frog 111-112

Climate 15, 21, 25-30, 44, 47, 51, 56-57, 61, 69, 73, 75, 77-78, 93, 125, 130, 132

Compost 38, 44-45, 60, 75, 78, 90, 95-96, 105, 123-125, 132

  Compost tea 90

Corms 27, 77-80, 141

Corralling 92

Cover Crops 44, 124, 127-130

Crop Planning   51-52, 63

Dahlias   13, 19, 27, 57, 59, 62, 75-76, 86, 92-93, 95, 97-98, 107, 111, 115, 119, 130-131, 141

Dampening Off   69-71

Deadheading   60, 76, 101, 104-105

Diseases   35, 45, 60, 76, 78, 89, 93, 95, 97, 124

Drip irrigation   75-76, 80, 89, 95, 124, 142

Fertilizing   33, 42, 75, 78, 90, 142

Flower Food   101, 103-104, 107-108, 111-112, 121, 132, 142-143

Frost Dates   29-30, 55

Garden Chores   132

Hardening Off   72

Hardiness Zones   25-26, 30

Harvesting   51, 53, 59, 62, 101-105

Hoop House   77-78, 80, 142

Hydration   103

Irrigation   35, 73, 75-76, 80, 89, 95, 124, 132, 142

Landscape Fabric   78, 80, 85-86, 89, 124, 128-129, 142

Mulch   44, 75, 86

Netting   76, 91, 123, 142

Perennials   26, 29, 86

Pests   33, 75, 83, 96-97, 143

Pinching   75, 92-93, 104

Planting   25, 30, 37, 44, 47-48, 52-53, 55, 60-63, 67-80, 85, 89-90, 96, 129-130

   Planning   26, 47-64, 51-53, 62-63, 67

   Spacing   47-48, 61, 75, 80

   Succession   60-61, 52, 55, 93-95

Preparation   33-45, 129-130

Pruning   132, 136

Postharvest   123-132

Ranunculus   27, 57, 59, 62, 77-80, 141

Seedlings   54, 63, 68-73, 83, 85, 89

   Hardening Off   72

   Starting   68-71

   Planting   54, 71-73

Seeds   15, 27, 37, 47, 51-54, 56, 63-64, 67-70, 76, 79, 101, 104, 128, 141

   Ordering   47, 63-64

Seed starting   54, 67, 69-70, 79, 142

Soil   33-34, 36-45, 60, 69-75, 78-80, 83, 86, 90, 95-96, 123-124, 127-131, 142

Staking   48, 53, 74, 76, 83, 92, 136

Succession   52, 55, 60-61, 93, 95

Succession Planting   60-61, 52, 55, 93-95

Testing   40-42, 44, 90

Tools   33, 36, 47, 67, 72, 80, 83, 86, 101, 107, 111, 115, 119, 123, 132, 136, 141-143

Transplanting   29, 51, 54-55, 71-72, 83

Tubers   27, 51, 75, 130-131, 141

Tulips   27, 60, 62, 64, 73

Watering   35, 70-71, 73-76, 80, 83, 89, 95

ss Zone Map

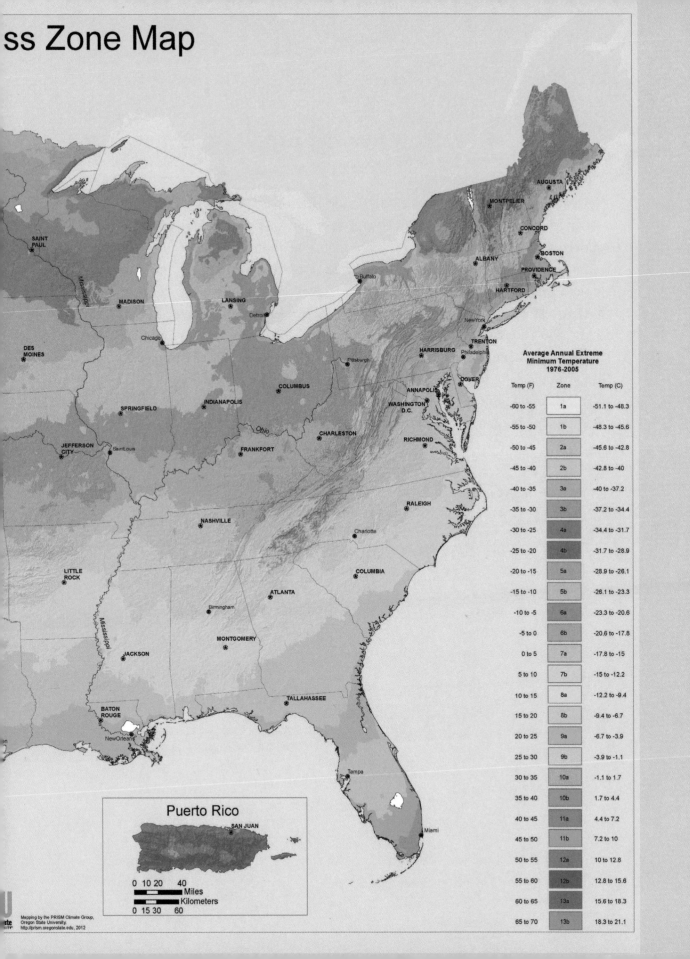

Average Annual Extreme Minimum Temperature 1976-2005

Temp (F)	Zone	Temp (C)
-60 to -55	1a	-51.1 to -48.3
-55 to -50	1b	-48.3 to -45.6
-50 to -45	2a	-45.6 to -42.8
-45 to -40	2b	-42.8 to -40
-40 to -35	3a	-40 to -37.2
-35 to -30	3b	-37.2 to -34.4
-30 to -25	4a	-34.4 to -31.7
-25 to -20	4b	-31.7 to -28.9
-20 to -15	5a	-28.9 to -26.1
-15 to -10	5b	-26.1 to -23.3
-10 to -5	6a	-23.3 to -20.6
-5 to 0	6b	-20.6 to -17.8
0 to 5	7a	-17.8 to -15
5 to 10	7b	-15 to -12.2
10 to 15	8a	-12.2 to -9.4
15 to 20	8b	-9.4 to -6.7
20 to 25	9a	-6.7 to -3.9
25 to 30	9b	-3.9 to -1.1
30 to 35	10a	-1.1 to 1.7
35 to 40	10b	1.7 to 4.4
40 to 45	11a	4.4 to 7.2
45 to 50	11b	7.2 to 10
50 to 55	12a	10 to 12.8
55 to 60	12b	12.8 to 15.6
60 to 65	13a	15.6 to 18.3
65 to 70	13b	18.3 to 21.1

Puerto Rico

SAN JUAN

0 10 20 40
Miles
Kilometers
0 15 30 60

Mapping by the PRISM Climate Group,
Oregon State University,
http://prism.oregonstate.edu, 2012

yellow pear 🍐 press

Yellow Pear Press, established in 2015, publishes inspiring, charming, clever, distinctive, playful, imaginative, beautifully designed lifestyle books, cookbooks, literary fiction, notecards, and journals with a certain joie de vivre in both content and style. Yellow Pear Press books have been honored by the Independent Publisher Book (IPPY) Awards, National Indie Excellence Awards, Independent Press Awards, and International Book Awards. Reviews of our titles have appeared in Kirkus Reviews, Foreword Reviews, Booklist, Midwest Book Review, San Francisco Chronicle, and New York Journal of Books, among others. Yellow Pear Press joined forces with Mango Publishing in 2020, both with the vision to continue publishing clever and innovative books. The fact that they're both named after fruit is a total coincidence.

We love hearing from our readers, so please stay in touch with us and follow us at:

Facebook: Yellow Pear Press

Instagram: @yellowpearpress

Pinterest: yellowpearpress

Website: www.mangopublishinggroup.com